O9-BHJ-510

THE HAPLESS HANDYMAN'S

HOME REPAIR
AND
WEEKEND PROJECT GUIDE

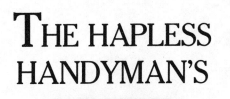

THE HAPLESS HANDYMAN'S

HOME REPAIR AND WEEKEND PROJECT GUIDE

SONNY "BUBBA" FERGUSON

with illustrations by SCRAWLS

Rutledge Hill Press
Nashville, Tennessee

Copyright © 1992 Don O'Briant and Sam C. Rawls

All rights reserved. Written permission must be secured from the publisher to use or reproduce any part of this book, except for brief quotations in critical reviews or articles.

Published in Nashville, Tennessee, by Rutledge Hill Press, 513 Third Avenue South, Nashville, Tennessee 37210. Distributed in Canada by H. B. Fenn & Company, Ltd., Mississauga, Ontario.

Typography by D&T/Bailey, Nashville, Tennessee

Library of Congress Cataloging-in-Publication Data

Ferguson, Sonny Bubba, 1943–
     The hapless handyman's home repair and weekend project guide /
Sonny "Bubba" Ferguson   ;   with illustrations by Sam Rawls.
        p.   cm.
     ISBN 1-55853-199-8
     1. Dwellings—Maintenance and repair—Amateurs' manuals.
I. Rawls, Sam, 1940–   . II. Title.
TH4817.3.F47   1992
643'.7—dc20   92-28585
                                                                                       CIP

Printed in the United States of America
1 2 3 4 5 6 7 8 — 98 97 96 95 94 93 92

CONTENTS

INTRODUCTION

Right now you are probably thinking, what on earth do I need with another home repair book? I already have the complete Time-Life *Encyclopedia of Woodworking,* the *Readers' Digest Comprehensive Home Repair Manual,* and Jimmy Swaggart's *Guide to Gutters and Bedrooms.*

That may be true, but the question is: Have you ever read any of those dull books with all the complicated drawings? Sure, they look pretty on the shelf along with that set of encyclopedias you bought just before your son dropped out of eighth grade and became an assistant carnival barker for the Snake Lady sideshow. And they're mighty impressive when your father-in-law is visiting and starts browsing through your books. But they might as well be instructions for building the B-1 bomber for all the good you're getting out of them.

Let's face it. We would all like to build nice furniture for our spouses, but most of us have trouble following even the simplest directions in those how-to books. (Isn't the clock on your VCR still flashing?) The reason is very simple. These books are written by *people who know what they're doing.* These people are *professionals.* Try asking a neurosurgeon how he performs an operation, and he'll look at you like you need a little cranial work yourself. "It's too complicated," he'll say.

Too complicated. That's easy for him to say. He's never had to try to put together a metal utility shed with a regular screwdriver when all the screws have Phillips heads. He's never tried to replace the grease trap in a leaky kitchen sink. And he most certainly has never had to cut crown molding to fit corners.

Performing a prefrontal lobotomy is a piece of cake compared to some of the repairs homeowners face on a regular basis. And God forbid if you have to call in a repairman. Have you ever wondered how the guy who fixes your toilet is able to buy his wife a new Cadillac every two years?

In these recessionary times, more and more of us are becoming do-it-yourselfers. Or attempt-it-yourselfers. The sad fact is, most of us are hapless when it comes to any power tool more complicated than a blender. We waste a half-day on Saturday disassembling the kitchen sink, spend $67.50 on strange-looking wrenches and PVC pipe, and still end up calling the plumber literally to bail us out.

Just the other day I was trying to catch the last quarter of an NFL playoff game on TV when my wife came in, turned down the volume, and stood in front of the set with her arms crossed. I knew right away that she wanted to have a discussion.

"Your daughter wants you to build her a tree house in the back yard."

"She's fourteen now," I said. "Isn't she interested in boys yet?"

"No, she wants a tree house. You promised her a tree house."

"Yes, but that was when she was eight. I just never got around to it. I'll start on it first thing in the morning," I whined. My wife gently suggested that I'd better get to Home Depot and pick up some materials if I didn't want my poker buddies to see those pictures of me in her blue pantyhose.

"But that was a Halloween outfit," I protested. "I was dressed as Superman."

"I believe you," she said. "But will Roy Bill, Earl, and Junior?"

Well, four weekends and five mashed fingers later, I had constructed something that looked like the Maginot Line in a pine tree.

"What's that?" my daughter asked when I proudly showed her my handiwork.

"It's a tree house."

"No, it's not. It looks like a tornado picked up a pile of boards and flung them into the tree. I'm not climbing into that thing."

"It doesn't look very sturdy," my wife observed.

"Sturdy?" I protested. "Why, I used 8-penny nails and 1 x 4s. It's strong enough to hold six or eight grown men."

"You try it," my wife said.

I may be a shoddy craftsman, but I'm no fool. I called Lester, the sixteen-year-old blimp from next door and told him I had left a meat-lovers supreme pizza in the tree house. Three minutes later, Lester came tumbling down faster than the Berlin Wall.

"I told you it wasn't safe," my wife said as my daughter fled into the house in tears.

"I couldn't find the pizza," Lester said, setting the west

wall of the tree house aside and picking splinters out of his rear end.

The next weekend I watched while a guy with the name *Bob* on his coveralls erected a fortress with a roof in my backyard. He used pressure-treated 4 x 4s, 4 x 6s, and 2 x 6s and fastened them with large bolts. When he left with six hundred dollars of my money, my daughter scampered up the ladder with two of her friends and disappeared into a room that was more spacious than my den.

"Why couldn't you have done that?" my wife asked.

"There's a very good reason," I explained. "I'm a klutz."

And so are most men. We are the poor guys who are summoned whenever a faucet starts to leak or a wooden step rots or a window needs replacing. Wives automatically assume we are as capable with tools as their fathers were. Well, their fathers didn't have to put up with traffic jams and computer viruses and other ills of the modern work world. They grew up with tools. Their fathers taught them how to build things. Our fathers, with a few exceptions, did not.

Instruction manuals and projects books don't help much either. If we could figure out blueprints, we wouldn't need those books in the first place. What do all those arrows and dotted lines mean anyway? Why couldn't there be a guide for totally inept craftsmen?

Well now there is. In preparing *The Hapless Handyman's Home Repair and Weekend Project Guide,* I have tried to follow a time-proven system of doing things that is even simpler than the Shaker method: The White Trash Way. There are no fancy curves or dadoes to cut, no intricate molding to cut, and, best of all, low costs. In most cases scrap materials can be used and assembled with a few primitive tools. If more sophisticated power equipment is required, it can easily be obtained from one of your neighbors who has a pegboard tool rack in his workshop along with individual containers for each size screw and nail. Just remember to return the tools promptly, or else store them in a clean, dry place until you need them again or your neighbor comes looking for them.

With this hapless handyman's guide, you'll astound your neighbors and impress your wife. You'll save thousands of dollars avoiding needless repairs and making cheap, worthless knickknacks for your in-laws' Christmas presents.

If ever there was a man who needed this book, it's my

friend Roy Bill Cole. I was over at Roy Bill's house the other night when the subject of woodworking came up. Roy Bill had just bought another bookcase to store all of his how-to books. He had everything from *Backyard Projects* to *Build Your Own Wooden Boat.* Unfortunately, Roy Bill is the only person I know who failed high-school shop. He tried to build a few bluebird houses several years ago, but they were so shoddy they were condemned by the bluebird housing inspectors. He couldn't even get a family of ruby-necked white thrashers to move in.

"What ever happened to that harvest table you were going to build for Eleanor?" I asked.

Roy Bill shifted his recliner into another position and reached for a cold beer on top of a stack of home repair guides. "I'm waiting for the wood to season."

"How long have you been waiting?"

"Sixteen years." He took another sip of beer and looked up at the blank TV screen. The remote control was perched on top of the set.

"How much longer do you have to wait?" I, too, noticed the remote control but was not about to leave my seat by the fire.

"A few months. You start working with that pine when it's too moist, and them boards will warp on you."

"I can understand that," I said.

"Planning," Roy Bill said. "Measure twice, cut once."

"Absolutely."

"Honey," Roy Bill shouted into the kitchen, where his wife Eleanor was preparing a nouvelle cuisine dish of poached catfish à la Charles and grits soufflé. "Would you mind handing me the remote control? I think the Falcons are on TV."

Twenty minutes later Roy Bill and I found a corner booth at Manuel's Tavern and settled down to watch the game.

"I don't believe I've ever seen Eleanor that mad," I said during a commercial.

"She'll get over it," Roy Bill said with the conviction of a man who had spent more time in the doghouse than Rin Tin Tin.

"I don't know. Why'd she dump all your clothes out by the street?"

"Goodwill truck is coming tomorrow." He popped two aspirins and washed them down with a Lite beer. "Well, I guess I'll go ahead and make that harvest table. That wood ought to be seasoned enough, don't you think?"

"As seasoned as it's ever going to be."

There is a reasonably happy ending to this story. Four weekends and hundreds of wasted dollars later, Roy Bill hauled his feeble effort to the dump and went by the Wood-U-Finish store to buy a ready-made harvest table. His father-in-law sanded and stained it. Now Eleanor seems relatively satisfied. But as for Roy Bill, I don't think he will ever get over the humiliation of having to watch a TV without remote control.

All of Roy Bill's troubles (well, his woodworking ones, anyway) could have been avoided if he had had access to *The Hapless Handyman's Home Repair and Weekend Project Guide.* Maybe the harvest table would not have looked as fancy as the one Roy Bill bought at the Wood-U-Finish place, but it would have been built with his own two hands. And most women will tell you that means more than all the Queen Anne furniture in the world.

There are no complicated blueprints in *The Hapless Handyman's Home Repair and Weekend Project Guide.* No tricky cuts. No exotic instructions. In fact, these directions are so simple, even your brother-in-law can follow them. But for goodness' sake, don't let him near your power saw when there are children or small animals in the vicinity. I still remember what happened to Uncle Earl's beagle when his brother-in-law Lamar was building a doghouse. Believe me, it was not a pretty picture.

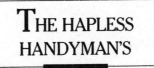

THE HAPLESS HANDYMAN'S

HOME REPAIR
AND
WEEKEND PROJECT GUIDE

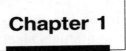

Chapter 1

A MAN'S HOME IS HIS CASTLE . . . AND OTHER MYTHS

HOME IMPROVEMENT was invented shortly after prehistoric women got tired of living in trees and lured their mates into caves. Until then, prehistoric men were basically happy nomads who went out in groups and brought back hairy dead animals. Then they sat around the campfire and told lies about their hunting exploits.

At first, the men were relatively content in the caves. Things were a little smoky until they discovered chimneys, but living conditions were an improvement over sleeping on a limb beneath a sixteen-foot python.

Not long after the men got used to curling up by the fire in the nice snug cave, one of the women decided the square boulder would look better in the spot where the round boulder was situated. And wouldn't it be more civilized if they painted a few pictures on the walls? As a matter of fact, why not knock a hole through that wall to connect it with the adjoining cave? Unfortunately, sometimes there were large animals sleeping in the adjoining cave, and that's where the term *den* originated.

Scientists who appeared on "Geraldo" recently maintained that prehistoric men walked upright before they moved into caves, but all that stooping and lifting affected their posture for thousands of years until the *chiropractus manipulatus* appeared.

Things haven't improved much since our ancestors began building thatched huts. Modern man doesn't go out every day and stalk his food unless he's a lawyer, but he is still expected to take care of every household disaster that occurs. Never mind that he doesn't know the difference between a ratchet and a rabbet; he's the man, and he's supposed to take care of these things.

Left alone, men would live in a house for thirty or forty years without changing a thing except the TV channel. Not the sheets, not the wallpaper, and most certainly not the furnace filter. That's because men are still basically nomads and women are nest builders.

Once a man has been lured into a house by his new bride, he is doomed. Initially, there are pictures to be hung and curtain rods to be installed. Pretty simple stuff if you've got a hammer. It's a little more difficult trying to drive a ½-inch tack into the wall with a rusty monkey wrench.

Maintaining a house properly leaves little time for the really important things in life, such as eating, sleeping, watching reruns of "The Waltons" on TV, and teaching your dog to fetch the remote control.

Now there are books that tell you what to do each month to keep your house in shape. That's right. A sea-

sonal checklist. As if we didn't have enough to worry about what, with Bob Vila being taken off "This Old House" and Johnny Carson retiring. Now we have to be concerned with inspecting our roofs for wear and tear *before* they start leaking, replacing our toilet seats *before* they break, and patching cracks in our driveway *before* they get large enough to pose a hazard to nearsighted relatives and small, clumsy pets.

If you're the nervous type, I suppose there's nothing wrong with an ounce of prevention. But given the choice, most of us would prefer following my Uncle Jim's system of crisis management.

"If it ain't broke, don't fix it." That was his motto, and he was a skilled carpenter.

I remember one of the many times my Aunt Mae mentioned that one of the back steps was sagging.

"Is it broke?" my uncle asked. Then he lit up his third Camel and resumed watching Dizzy Dean announce the Indians–Yankees game on the black and white Zenith TV set.

"Well, no," my aunt replied.

"When it breaks, I'll fix it."

"What if somebody steps on it when it breaks?"

"I'll take care of that," he grumbled.

Uncle Jim's solution was to take the remainder of the can of green paint he had used on his boat and write "Watch Your Step" on the step.

That lasted about two days, or until he realized that Aunt Mae was never going to fry pork chops or make mashed potatoes and gravy until he replaced the step.

Even then, he complained about how the board still had a few good weeks of wear left in it.

As good a craftsman as my uncle was, he truly believed that you should listen to your house just as you listen to your car. When Uncle Jim's car started making funny noises, he took it to the garage. Until then, he never lifted the hood.

"That's what those gauges are for, son," he told me.

"Why go looking for trouble? You want a doctor poking around in you when you don't have any symptoms?"

Unfortunately, houses don't have gauges. So we have to be alert. Water dripping from the ceiling during a rainstorm is an indication that something is wrong somewhere. Until you can determine whether you have a leak or the neighbor's incontinent tomcat has crawled into the attic again, simply find a large pot, and position it squarely under the liquid nuisance.

At some point, your wife is going to suggest that you fix the roof. Ignore her. Unless you're Noah, the rain isn't going to last very long; and by the time the sun comes out again, the leak will be forgotten until the next downpour.

If you're truly conscientious, you'll climb into the attic and dispose of the tomcat, or drive a nail upward through the roof to mark the spot of the leak. Later, when it's safe to climb onto the roof, apply some tar or replace the faulty shingle, and glue it down according to your father-in-law's instructions as he stands on the ground thirty feet away and shouts advice.

WARNING SIGNS FOR HOMEOWNERS

- You can lie in bed at night and count the stars—and you don't have a skylight.
- Aluminum siding salesmen abruptly stop calling.
- Chewing sounds inside the walls drown out Roseanne (Barr) Arnold's voice on Tuesday night.
- Your wife's favorite squash casserole dish slides off the kitchen table because the floor slopes at a thirty-degree angle.
- The lights flicker when you plug in Mr. Coffee.®
- It takes three days for your bathtub to drain.

- The outside of your house matches the colors of Tonto's horse.
- Your household pets begin acting nervous and eventually flee into the neighbor's yard.

Chapter 2

THERE'S NO TOOL LIKE A BORROWED TOOL

(Setting Up Your Shop on a Shoestring)

A WELL-STOCKED TOOLBOX and properly organized workshop are essential for the handyman, even a hapless one. That's why it is very important when you are buying a new house to check out your neighbors carefully. If one of them has a separate garage with pegboard paneling, shelves, little jars with all the screws and nails labeled, and a complete set of power tools, go ahead and close the deal. So what if your wife doesn't like the wallpaper and there's only one bathroom. You won't get many opportunities like this one. Living next door to someone with the proper tools is worth thousands of dollars.

Of course, don't expect to walk right over the first day and borrow your neighbor's router. There are strict rules of etiquette involved here.

- Start with something small, like a screwdriver, and work your way up the tool chain until you have free access to his radial arm saw.
- Return the small tools promptly to lull him into a false sense of security.
- Occasionally bring him freshly baked pies and cakes to prove that you are a good neighbor.
- Leave baskets of zucchini and tomatoes on his back porch during the summer (If you don't have a garden, don't worry; get these vegetables from your other neighbors in exchange for letting them use your borrowed tools).
- Pass along strategic bits of information, such as, "Gee, Fred, I didn't know your wife was such good friends with the mailman," or "Gosh, Fred, where does your wife put all those snacks? The Charles Chips® man stops by every day and stays for hours." You may lose a perfectly good neighbor, but you can really pick up bargains at those garage sales after a messy divorce.

If you're not the sort of fellow who believes in borrowing things, you can ignore the above advice and actually *buy* your own tools. Just be forewarned: You can get a hamburger franchise for about the same investment you make in a good shop. Or at least take a two-week family vacation to Wakulla Springs, Panama City, Florida, or Ross Allen's Reptile Farm.

But if you're determined to spend your money, here are

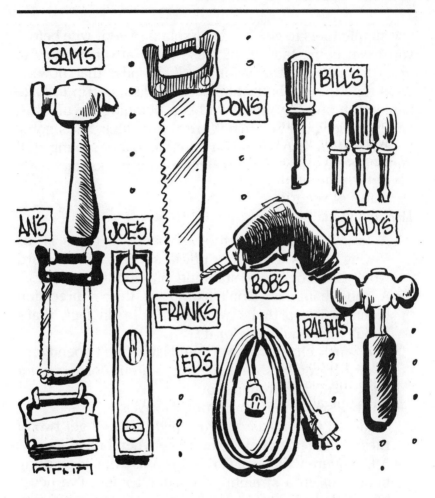

some suggestions for the basic shop. The first thing you'll need is a good workbench. You could build your own, but if you're that good, you wouldn't be reading this book. Go buy one of the kits at a building supply warehouse (get one that has a vise) along with a Workmate and two sawhorse kits. While you're there, you'll need to pick up a few simple tools to get started. Explain to your wife before you leave home that all of these tools are necessary in order to make life easier for her. If she buys that, now's a good time to ask about that weekend fishing trip to Lake Lanier you and Roy Bill have been planning for months. Well, maybe you'd better not press your luck. She's going to be upset enough when you dump all of her sewing stuff out of the garage to make room for your workshop.

THE TOOL LIST

- A 15-inch all-purpose toolbox handsaw (This is for sawing boards when your power saw's extension cord won't reach or you're standing in a puddle of water).
- A good hammer (Don't skimp on this; a precision hammer is worth its weight in gold. In fact, that's about what you'll pay for it).
- A 7¼-inch circular power handsaw (Don't spend less than forty dollars for this. You can cut corners a lot easier with a well-made tool).
- A sabre saw (great for cutting sabres).
- A 25-foot tape measure (You might as well get two of these, since I can never find mine when I need it).
- A tri-square with level (I think you use this for cutting boards off in a straight line; I don't know. I've never been able to do it. The level part is used by craftsmen who are bothered by buildings that lean a little. If that doesn't bother you, don't concern yourself with this piece of equipment).
- A variable speed ⅜-inch reversible drill with disc sanding attachment (No, Lamar, I don't think the reversible part means it fills up the hole if you make a

mistake, but that sanding attachment sure comes in handy when you're preparing the pick-up for another coat of Bondo).

- An assortment of drill bits
- A utility knife
- A set of screwdrivers, regular and Phillips head (The Phillips head is the one that has a little cross on the end).
- Screwdriver bits for your drill (This is real handy for screwing screws into hard wood).
- A set of chisels
- A variable speed jigsaw
- A variable speed sander
- A pry bar (great for removing nails and unsticking windows).
- A hacksaw
- Vise-grip pliers
- Regular pliers
- An adjustable crescent wrench (If heavy enough, it can be used to drive nails or knock down loose boards, but mainly it is used to tighten crescents).
- Four adjustable wood clamps
- A bevel gauge
- A good table saw with stand
- A drill press on a floor stand
- A router with stand and assortment of bits (This is a handy device that is used to destroy the edges of wood. In the proper hands, it makes nice designs, cuts grooves, and trims laminates. So if you have a shaggy laminate, this is the tool for you).
- A couple of store-bought toolboxes big enough to carry the portable tools (Or you can do like Lamar

and just get a couple of five-gallon buckets and dump everything in).
- Various kinds of safety equipment, including:

  - Safety goggles
  - Safety mask
  - Mouth guard
  - Elbow pads
  - Chest protector
  - Shin guards
  - Steel-toed boots
  - Leather gloves
  - Hard hat
  - Plastic cup athletic protector (You can't be too careful when it comes to preserving your valuable tools).

- Assortment of nails, screws, washers, poker chips, potato chips, and ashtrays (self-explanatory).
- Optional items, including:

  - Foam beverage holders (Dehydration is one of the major problems facing woodworkers).
  - Portable TV and AM/FM Radio (for use while you're waiting for the glue to dry on pieces of furniture).
  - Chain saw (for those stubborn cuts and persistent household pests).

As you can see, all of this calls for a substantial investment. So you can go ahead and set up a workshop in your garage or outbuilding, or you can continue to borrow tools from your neighbor or father-in-law and spend the money on something more worthwhile, like a big-screen TV. Just remember, while you're sipping a cold beer and watching the Giants and the Bears playing, you could be out in the workshop making priceless keepsakes for your family. Imagine the flush of joy on your wife's face when she discovers a broom-handle paper towel holder under the Christmas tree or unwraps that double-wide purple martin house on her anniversary. On second thought, if you do decide to go with the workshop, I suggest making an extra-large doghouse first. Yes, I know you don't have a dog, but you'll thank me later—especially when your wife finds out her canning jars are being used to store rusty 20-penny nails.

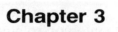
They Laughed When I Picked Up My Hammer

(How to Tell If You're a Hapless Handyman)

BEFORE YOU BEGIN any home repairs or woodworking projects, it helps to determine your skill level. This is kind of like finding your golf handicap. That way you won't tackle a job that's too complicated, get frustrated, and quit. Success breeds success. Complete a project—no matter how simple—and your confidence grows.

So be honest and see if any of the following applies to you.

You know you're a hapless handyman if:

- You think a mitered joint is something Bill Clinton smoked in college.
- The only tools you've owned are a complete set of Ginsu knives.

- The clerk at the lumberyard asks you how long you want your 2 x 4s and you say "several years."
- You took Latin instead of shop in high school.
- You buy all of your kids' toys preassembled for Christmas—even Mr. Potato Head.
- You have to hire a plumber to caulk your bathtub.
- Your hammer costs less than a Happy Meal at McDonald's.
- The most-used items in your toolbox are baling wire and duct tape.
- You have used a crescent wrench to drive nails.
- You think a plumb bob is one of the Waltons.
- Every line you've ever sawed looks like the southern border of Afghanistan.
- You think the reverse switch on your electric drill is used to fill in holes you drilled by mistake.
- Your newest piece of sandpaper was bought before Elvis died.
- The only staples you've handled have been in a *Playboy* centerfold's tummy.
- Your wife asks you for a coat rack and you drive four 20-penny nails in a row on the wall.
- You wear suspenders, your pants fit, and none of your shirts has your first name stitched above the pocket.
- You have no idea what those little marks between the numbers on your tape measure are for.
- You try to haul sheetrock on the roof of your Saab.
- Your work shoes are scuffed Weejuns.
- You buy bandages in bulk.
- The ugly, overweight, lonely widow next door quits asking you for help.

- You think a nail apron is something Madge the Manicurist wears.
- You're not sure, but you think soffit is something you do with gravy.
- You need help changing the furnace filter.
- You think a dado is a marital aid.

Maybe you're not guilty of all of these, but if you checked off more than two or three, chances are you are a prime candidate for *The Hapless Handyman's Home Repair and Weekend Project Guide.* It's nothing to be ashamed of. Look at Bob what's-his-name, who used to host "This Old House" on PBS. Bob would wander around, stepping in wet concrete, following Norm the carpenter and asking the stupidest questions. Norm, who is both competent and polite, would try to answer them as simply as possible. Bob would listen intently, turn to the audience, and repeat what Norm had said, then ask the same thing on the next show.

"Why are you nailing that board there, Norm?"

"This is called a step, Bob."

"And I suppose you'll be adding another one just above that one."

"That's right, Bob."

"And this goes into this room here. What is it going to be?"

"The kitchen, Bob."

"Is that why you're installing cabinets and a sink in there?"

"That's right, Bob. We tried putting the cabinets and sink and stove in a small room several hundred yards from the house, but we find this is much more efficient."

Take a lesson from Bob and never be afraid to ask questions, even dumb ones. When I was growing up, my father and my uncle (both carpenters) came home all sweaty and smelling of sawdust and talked excitedly about the houses they were building. I was so smart then, I didn't need to ask questions. Besides, if anything ever needed doing, even after I had a family of my own, I just called my father and asked him to visit for a weekend. And bring his toolbox.

He's gone now, and I've had to learn everything the hard way. But one thing I've discovered is that you can always ask questions. The first thing you should do when you move into a new house or a new neighborhood is to find the best hardware store in the area. Then make friends with the owner. He'll be glad to tell you which tools you'll need, what supplies, and which professional repairman to call once you botch the job. That's probably the most important part. You can find repairmen in the phone book, but sometimes you're taking a big chance. A repairman who is recommended by your local hardware manager is more than likely going to be honest and proficient. If he's not, tell the hardware store owner. Enough complaints, and he'll stop recommending him.

In the meantime, if you're determined to tackle some of these jobs yourself, don't be disappointed if the first ones don't turn out right. The first waffles are never very good, just like your first sexual encounters as a teenager. You're still eating waffles, aren't you? And you didn't quit having sex just because things were a little awkward at first.

Be bold. Strap on that tool apron. Unfurl that tape measure. Rev up that electric drill. Pick up that hammer and hold it as if you mean business. So what if your family and friends laugh? They laughed at Lamar Lawson and Wesley Simmons when they were teenagers (with good reason) and look what happened. Wesley has his own goat farm, and Lamar is one of the best Roto Rooter men in the business. You see what happens when you have a dream and follow it?

Chapter 4

Dadoes, Rabbets, and Other Endangered Wildlife

(Learning the Language)

REMEMBER HOW EMBARRASSED you used to be when you were helping your father fix something and he said, "Son, hand me that ¾-inch double-turreted hex nut straightener," and you searched through the pile of tools and handed him a ⅝-inch single-barreled propane catfish scorcher by mistake. Hey, it could happen to anyone. Only an expert would be able to tell the two tools apart. But you were young then, almost eighteen, and your father's reaction was always devastating.

"Not that one, dummy. I said I wanted the ¾-inch double-turreted hex nut straightener, not the ⅝-inch single-barreled propane catfish scorcher. Tell your sister to come out here and help me. You're about as smart as a bucket of bolts."

You know now that he didn't mean it. (Did you, Dad? Huh?) Mom was probably having a bad day and taking it out on Dad, which is why he was trying to fix the motor on the washing machine instead of calling a repairman. And maybe he just finished mashing his finger in a pair of snapping-turtle vise grips and was a little cross. And after all, didn't he make it up to you later by letting you sit under the steering wheel of his '56 Buick ("You turn on that ignition and you're dead meat") while he went into Ralph's Road House to see a man about a dog for two hours? And didn't he take you snipe hunting that night? No, I never could get those birds to run into my croaker sack either, no matter how long I stood out there in the dark.

Well, that's all history now, but you can avoid the embarrassment of not knowing the proper names of tools and things by memorizing the following glossary (a glossary is a small South American rodent that's real shiny):

- *Awl.* Now this depends on where you live. If you live south of the Mason-Dixon line, and somebody says, "Will that be awl?" it means "Will there be anything else?" An awl is a tool used to make a hole.
- *Auger,* as in "He auger not have done that." A drill bit that is used to bore holes.
- *Batten,* as in "The Braves are behind 3–1, but they're still batten." A narrow strip of wood used to cover cracks, such as on a board-and-batten structure.
- *Chamfer,* as in "That boy's just chamfering at the bit." In woodworking, it means a bevel.

- *Collet Chuck,* as in "MayNelle's oldest boy ate six hamburgers last night, and he got the awfulest case of the collet chuck." Actually, it's part of a wood lathe used to hold small round pieces of wood.
- *Concave.* A place where escaped prisoners hole up. It means something that's hollowed out.
- *Dado.* No, it has nothing to do with that, Lamar. This is a groove that's cut across the grain of a board.

- *Dowel.* A round peg. Usually it fits in a round hole.
- *Jack Plane.* A tool used to shave wood flat. Honest.
- *Miter.* "We miter won, but Lonzo got caught off second base." Connecting two pieces of wood both cut evenly at a 45-degree angle.
- *Ogee,* as in, "Ogee, Roy Bill, did you see the dadoes on that blonde?" Actually, a type of molding.
- *Rip Saw.* A powerful, sharp power tool used to cut wood with the grain. Or fingers in any direction.
- *Router.* Either someone who delivers the mail in the country, or a power tool used to cut grooves and make all kinds of designs on wood.
- *Screwdriver.* A drink made of orange juice and vodka, which you imbibe before looking for your screwdriver, which you misplaced six years ago and need now to fix the toaster.
- *Tail Vise.* Nope, I'm not going to touch this one. In woodworking, it's a contraption at the end of a workbench used to hold planks while you plane them.
- *Tape Measure.* A retractable metal ruler that is used to calculate lengths and widths inaccurately.
- *Yankee Screwdriver.* A tool purchased up north that makes screwing things up real easy.

Oh, and by the way, a *rabbet* is not a furry creature that brings Easter eggs. It's a groove cut in the edge of a board so that another piece can be fitted into it to form a joint.

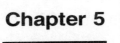
How to Control Skyrocketing Repair Costs

(Why You Should Trade Your Skyrocket)

BEN CASEY OR BEN FRANKLIN or one of those Bens once said, "An ounce of prevention is worth a pound of cure." He was right. Have you priced a pound of cure lately? Even figuring in the inflation index and the fact that the Japanese have cornered the market on widgets and microprocessors, it is still a staggering figure: $814.17. And the sad part is, a pound of cure just won't go as far as it used to. Why, to repair a normal-sized deck takes two or three pounds of cure. And that's not counting the water seal and the medical bills after you drop one of the 4 x 4s on your neighbor's kid's foot.

No, there are only five ways to save money on home repairs.

- Rent, don't buy.
- Move frequently and sell your house to desperate, soon-to-retire Yankees who have been living in Buffalo.
- Marry a handyman's daughter (or son).
- Ignore the problem.
- Use preventive maintenance.

The last option is probably the wisest, even if you have always believed like my Uncle Jim that if it ain't broke don't fix it. Now, I'm not the sort of fellow (like my father-in-law) who constantly prowls around his house looking for signs of trouble. I followed him on a recent visit, and he climbed into the attic, crawled under the house (I know why they call it a crawl-space, and I also know why you couldn't pay me to go under there with all those spiders and bugs), and went up on the roof to inspect everything from floor joists to shingles.

"I think I'll recaulk next week," he said, scribbling in his notepad. "And I'd better add another layer of insulation in the attic before winter."

More insulation! This is a man who has a whole zoo full of pink panthers (remember the TV commercial, folks) crammed in his attic. And he wants more. I still have two rolls in my attic that I bought after the ice storm of 1973 and haven't put down yet. Talk about itchy! If you don't wear long-sleeve shirts and gloves and a protective mask, it's worse than rolling in poison ivy.

And caulking. My father-in-law buys it by the case and

plugs every tiny crack in his house. I only use it when a neighbor complains that one of his kittens is missing or I notice large bats flying in and out at night.

But my father-in-law has the right idea. Caulking is much cheaper than replacing a wall. Waterproofing and using treated wood are a lot less expensive than building a new porch or deck. So now's the time to overcome your procrastination (no, Lamar, that's not what causes blindness) and get started.

GUTTERS

If all you know about gutters is what you read in the newspaper stories about Jimmy Swaggart, pay attention. Gutters are those things that are nailed under the edges of your roof to catch the water. They also catch leaves, straw, and anything else that blows onto your roof. Then, when it rains, your downspouts are all clogged up, the gutters overflow and back up under your shingles, and pretty soon you've got a rotten mess.

There are people who will clean out your gutters for you, usually neighborhood teenagers who need money for a tune-up for their BMW. It's O.K. to use them if you make them sign a waiver that they won't sue you if they fall off the roof. And be sure to climb up the ladder and check after they say they've finished. Not that you don't trust them, you understand, but we all have been teenagers once (except Molly Ringwald, and she's been a teenager several times).

The best thing to do with gutters is to install snap-on, hinged gutter guards. This may cost you a little bit now, but it will save you a lot of trouble later. Plus, you'll never have to hire those teenagers again, the ones who leered at your daughter and who kept referring to your wife as Mrs. Robinson and inviting her to go for a spin in a car that didn't smell like McDonald's after a high-school football night.

ATTICS

The less said about attics, the better. How do we accumulate so much junk? And why do we keep it? I was rummaging around up there one day and found a box containing my kids' elementary school report cards and a fifth-grade geography book.

"Why are we keeping this?" I asked my wife.

"That's part of your children's heritage. These are precious memories."

"The fact that my son needs to try harder and made a B in conduct is a precious memory?"

"Wait until you're a grandfather. Then you'll appreciate it."

"So will the silverfish. What about this geography book? It's so outdated, it doesn't even have the outcome of World War II."

"We'll get rid of it when we have our garage sale."

A garage sale. For years, we have kept baby clothes and changing tables, stored paperback novels, and housed useless toys on the pretense that we're going to have a garage sale. When? If you are married to a pack rat, or are one yourself, you know what I mean. An attic should be a place where *interesting* things are stored, like old love letters, photographs, and catalogs from Frederick's of Hollywood. Well, maybe seasonal clothes and Christmas decorations belong up there too, but at least leave an alley to navigate through to check on the conditions of your roof, which is why we're up here in the first place.

Unless you have an electric light outlet up there, take a good flashlight and wear old clothes, as if you were going night-fishing for crappie at the Little River trestle. If your attic does not have flooring, you're in big trouble. This means you have to lay down boards (strong boards, like pieces of 3/4-inch plywood) to walk or crawl on, or else you have to make sure you step only on the ceiling joists and not in between. It also might help to wear a dust mask.

Using the flashlight, check the underside of the roof for signs of water stains. The best time to do this is right after a heavy rainstorm. If you spot one, follow the instructions in the chapter on roofs. By catching leaks early, you can prevent damage to ceilings and walls later. Plus, if you have a houseful of relatives who are getting on your nerves, checking the attic is a good excuse to get away for a few quiet hours. My grandfather used this technique on my grandmother a lot—only he didn't have an attic. He insisted it was necessary to walk down to the barn to feed the calf several times a day. Once there, he reached into the corncrib, pulled out his jug of moonshine, and had a healthy snort. My grandmother never understood why the calf was not fatter.

CHIMNEYS

A fireplace is a wonderful thing. It produces smoke in great quantities, sucks all of the warm air out of a room, and makes grown men and women beyond their physical prime want to strip naked and lie down on bearskin rugs.

There is nothing wrong with that, I suppose, if it keeps middle-aged couples out of restaurants on weekends so I

won't have so long to wait. But if you have a fireplace, chances are you also have a chimney. And chimneys can be trouble for anyone except Mary Poppins. They can get clogged with soot and creosote and even catch fire. That would be disastrous, especially if you're on the bearskin rug with your loved one (or somebody else's loved one) and are forced to run naked into the yard yelling, "Fire!"

Now how long do you think it would be before folks took you seriously if you did that?

Anyway, that can be prevented by not taking your clothes off and by regularly cleaning your chimney. If you don't want to pay a chimney sweep (and believe me, it's worth the trouble and cost), measure the inside of your flue (that's the pipe that runs up the chimney) and buy a chimney brush with extension handles. Seal off the fireplace with plastic sheeting and duct tape, climb on the roof, and begin cleaning. You'll also need a heavy-duty shop vacuum. See, I told you that you would be better off hiring a chimney sweep.

WALLS

My Uncle Jim's philosophy about walls was, "If they're still standing and the cracks are not large enough to admit good-sized snakes, leave them alone." If you have higher standards than that, it pays to check your walls on a seasonal basis. Are any of the boards loose? Are there any signs of rotting? Have any of the bricks come loose? How about the trim around your windows? The best thing to do is follow my father-in-law Warren's advice and caulk frequently with a good silicone caulking, one that expands with the weather. And paint your house before it resembles the color of Tonto's horse, which, as I recall, was kind of a mottled shade. Or was that Wild Bill Hickok's? I know it wasn't Trigger.

Portions of your walls that are in heavily shaded areas may become discolored with mildew or fungus. While this may be quite a topic of conversation at deck parties, you should take steps to correct the problem by renting a pressure washer and using a mildew remover (or make your own by adding one part laundry bleach with three parts warm water). When you repaint, there are mildew-prevention additives you can use in the paint. Check with your paint expert at the building supply or hardware store.

Also check window and door trim for problems such as cracking and gaps. Are your wood shutters beginning to sag? It happens to everybody. Use metal corner braces to fix this.

Are there signs of insect damage on wood siding? If so, check the chapter on roaches and rednecks. Otherwise, call a good exterminator.

On stucco walls, inspect for cracks or water damage, and reseal with a stucco patch compound.

Wash your walls periodically with a garden hose or a carwash brush that attaches to your hose. A solution of trisodium phosphate (available at most hardware stores) is great for removing stains and dirt. But wear rubber gloves and protective eyewear. This stuff is pretty strong.

WINDOWS AND DOORS

If your window frames or sashes are cracked and peeling, scrape and sand and repaint. Replace any broken or cracked panes. Measure accurately (on the inside, not outside), and get someone at the hardware store to cut the pane for you. Apply a ⅛-inch thin bead of window putty around the edge of the frame. Carefully place the pane in and wiggle it until it's seated against the putty. Push firmly against the edges (not too firmly). Use a screwdriver to push the glazier points (you did buy some of those at the store) into the sash to hold the pane in place. Three or four per side will do it. Add another bead of putty and use a putty knife to smooth it out in a tri-angular pattern, like on the other windows. Dip your putty knife in mineral spirts and slide it over the putty for a smooth finish. The next day, after it dries, you can paint it with a primer and then use a color to match the rest of the window. If you haven't painted in a while, you might consider redoing all of the windows. That way they'll match and your wife will think you're so clever she'll cook you a meat loaf using her mother's recipe. On second thought, you might want to wait to repaint.

INTERIOR WALLS

Doesn't everyone look at the walls, you say? Well, yes and no. To inspect them properly, you need to get down on your hands and knees and check the moldings and underneath the windows and in the corners where the spiders live. If all that's needed is a good dusting and vacuuming, you're in good shape.

FLOORS

Why do floors creak? Probably because they wouldn't be able to make scary movies without them. Or maybe it's something mothers invented a long time ago to keep their teenage children from sneaking in at night without waking them. Wood floors are going to squeak eventually, no matter how well they are crafted. If a board is loose, try counter-sinking a screw and filling in the hole with plastic wood. Resand and finish to match the rest of the floor. But that's a lot of trouble. If you have a basement and can reach the floor from beneath, screw a drywall screw into the floorboard through the subflooring (make sure it will not go all the way through). Use a 1¼-inch screw. Sometimes sprinkling talcum powder between the floorboards will stop the squeaking for a while. It sure worked with Mama's first cousin's nephew's baby.

BASEMENTS

Right after God promised Noah he wouldn't send any more floods, he added another requirement. Unfortunately, in modern translations, what God said was either garbled or omitted altogether. As Noah was admiring the rainbow and thanking God for promising not to send any more floods, God said, "And by the way, Noah. Thou shalt not build any basements unless thou art prepared for leaks."

There are two kinds of basements: those that leak a little bit and those that leak a lot. Yours doesn't leak, you say? Then either you live in an arid climate or you are plain lucky.

The main reason basements leak is that the surface outside was not graded properly. If the ground slopes toward the house, you can expect some leaking. If you have a brother-in-law with heavy equipment (and I'm talking about backhoes, not his beer belly), get him to regrade the lot to slope *away* from your basement. Otherwise, seek professional help and call your banker.

PLUMBING

Repairs are covered in the chapter called Clogged Drains and Leaky Pipes, but there are some things you can do to prevent disasters and big plumbing bills. One, make sure your septic tank is healthy. Pour some buttermilk down the drain periodically to help the action. Have the tank pumped out every five years or so, unless you belong to a family like Lamar's, in which case every six months would not be soon enough. Don't plant willow trees or bamboo near the septic tank drainage line. A sure sign of trouble with your septic tank is a foul odor combined with a slow-draining bathtub.

Water heaters are another potential source of trouble. Try draining a few gallons of water every five or six months to prevent build-up of sediment, which cuts down on the efficiency. Check your manual for instructions. If you can't find your manual, get your plumber to do it when he's there for another job.

The secret to saving money on home repairs is knowing when to call in a professional and when to do the job yourself. Don't tackle something you know is beyond your capabilities. But most preventive maintenance is something every able-bodied man and woman can learn to do. If you're still unsure of yourself, go ahead and hire a professional to do the maintenance and watch how it's done. Ask questions. And the next time you'll be able to do it yourself. Unless you're one of the Lawson boys, of course. Lanier Lawson came home from school one day and proudly announced to his father, Homer, that the teacher had told him he was the strongest boy in the fifth grade.

"Is it because I'm a Lawson, Daddy?" Lanier asked.

"No, son," Homer replied sadly, "it's because you're eighteen years old."

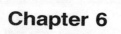

Chapter 6

"AS LONG AS THEY'RE HERE . . ."

(How to Deal with Contractors, Remodelers, and Other Natural Disasters)

ANYONE WHO HAS EVER had any remodeling work done knows the pitfalls. What begins as a simple job soon escalates into a full-scale project lasting weeks and costing thousands of dollars. The Taj Mahal probably started out as a small gazebo, and look what happened. I know it's tempting, once the crew has shown up, to get them to do a few other things. But those other things add up. Just ask Mama's sister-in-law's niece Velma.

Velma wanted a new handrail put up on the front steps because her daddy had a hip operation and couldn't climb without a little support. So she called Honest Clyde and the Nail-Driving Five (they pick up extra money at gospel singings on the weekends). She called them the week before Labor Day, and by Halloween they had already given her enough excuses to fill a Blue Horse notebook. Finally, Clyde and four of the Nail-Driving Five showed up the first week in November (Jim Frank had a sinus problem) and gave her an estimate.

"Three hundred dollars to put up a handrail?" Velma screamed.

"Uh, not exactly," Clyde backtracked. "I said, if you wanted to use the best materials, that's what it would cost."

"What are you going to use? Mahogany?" Velma said, her voice stripping paint off the rocker panel of Clyde's Ford.

"No, ma'am, I was going to use Philippine cedar. It lasts forever."

"Hell, Clyde, Daddy's already eighty-three. I don't need it to last forever."

Clyde eventually gave her a price of fifty-nine dollars for the handrail, but in the meantime he convinced her that she could use some new steps and a new porch.

"Well, as long as you're here," Velma said, "why don't you take a look at this squeaky board in the hall."

By the time Clyde and the Nail-Driving Five departed (Jim Frank showed up on Thursday), Velma had a new porch, new steps, new handrails, and new flooring in her hallway, all to the tune of $2,397.43.

"I can't explain it," she told her friend Wanda June. "I saw those men working and figured I might as well get a few other things fixed. The worst thing is, they're coming back at Easter to build me a deck."

Let me give you a word of advice here. When you and your "significant other" decide to remodel your house, and I hope you think long and hard before you decide to do that, sit down together at the kitchen table, tell the kids you're going to talk about sex so they'll leave you alone, and make certain you know what you both want.

If you want a new kitchen, fine, put in a new kitchen. You want a new kitchen and a new bathroom? Fine. But don't wait until the workmen start tearing down walls before you decide you want to add a second story to your house.

Once you have decided what you want and you have picked out the fixtures and cut out pictures from magazines, send your wife (or husband—whoever is the most susceptible to whimsy) out of town until the job is done. If something comes up while they're gone, their absence gives you a perfect excuse to postpone making a decision. The longer you wait, the more logical your decision will be. Follow the same precautions you do when you shop at the grocery store. Eat first, avoid impulse items, and buy only those things that are on your list.

OTHER TIPS:

- Use remodelers who have done work for people you know. Check out their workmanship and ask probing questions about what everything cost and if it was within their original estimate.
- Get everything, and I mean *everything,* in writing.
- Most contractors and home remodelers are honest, but they are in the business to make money. Don't pay them any more than is necessary.
- Check off what was done every day, and make sure they aren't cutting corners on materials or anything else.

- Set a deadline for having the job finished. There will be unavoidable delays, of course, but unless you have a reasonable timetable, a lot of remodelers will stretch your project out over weeks. It may not cost you any more in dollars, but the stress of living in limbo will take its toll in other ways. You may find yourself snapping at your cat, yelling at Girl Scouts who are peddling cookies, and eating several bags of corn chips and Famous Amos Chocolate Chip Cookies out of frustration.
- *If* they find something else that needs fixing, such as a rotten joist or a sagging rafter, get a separate estimate for that job. If you think the price is out of line, ask for another estimate from a different contractor.
- A rule of thumb on figuring renovations: Get three estimates. Add them together and double them, and that is reasonably close to what you'll end up paying.

A BIGGER PROBLEM

Paying for the job is not nearly as difficult as getting the craftsmen to show up in the first place. Where do they go? My friend Tinah Lynn was looking forward to cooking in her newly remodeled kitchen when all of a sudden the workmen disappeared for two days. When they came back, all they did was sweep up, install a couple of hinges, and leave again for another job.

"I just wish they'd go ahead and hook up the electricity and water so we can use the kitchen," she said. "And I can't get any kind of explanation out of the foreman. I'm not even sure he speaks English."

No, Tinah Lynn, he doesn't speak English. He speaks Contracting. And if you're going to deal with remodelers and such, you need to learn to speak Contracting, too. When a workman looks you squarely in the eye and tells you he'll have his crew out there the next morning, you can bet they'll either show up in the middle of the afternoon or first thing in the morning—a week from now.

"You said Tuesday," Tinah Lynn fumed when the crew arrived carrying picnic coolers of Dr. Peppers and ham sandwiches.

"It's Tuesday," the foreman said.

"I thought you meant last Tuesday."

"Tuesday is Tuesday. You want us to work? We work."

Four hours later they piled into the truck, leaving gaping holes in what was once her kitchen. "We have to check on another job. We'll be back later," the foreman said.

And so it went for nearly a month.

If Tinah Lynn and Velma knew how to speak Contracting, there would have been none of this frustration. In Contracting, time is meaningless except when it comes to figuring out their hourly pay. Most of these guys don't even own calendars. They have little notebooks that they make marks in with a number two pencil, and then they stick the notebooks in their pockets while they're working and they sweat and all of the writing fades. One contractor admitted to me that he was sure he had three jobs somewhere, but he'd forgotten where they were. He figured sooner or later somebody would call.

When a contractor leaves one job to check on another, that's exactly what he's doing. These guys are better jugglers than the acts on Ed Sullivan. In Famous Contractors School in Pueblo, Colorado, they teach them to never finish one job if it can be put off for a few days. They also

teach them the art of looking worried while talking in doublespeak about a little problem.

Take the case of poor Mrs. Eulalie Johnson of Plum Branch. Mrs. Eulalie is a widow on a fixed income, who decided to turn her carport into an apartment so her sister could come live with her.

About a week after the work commenced, the foreman approached Mrs. Johnson, who was watching "All My Children" on TV, and announced that he had a slight problem.

"Uh, Mrs. Johnson, you haven't seen your orange cat lately, have you?"

"Oh, not since breakfast yesterday morning," she said, smiling sweetly. "But Precious likes to roam around through the neighborhood sometimes. He may be old like me, but he's still a very active tomcat."

"Yes, ma'am, I know how that is, but what I'm trying to tell you is that J. W., he thinks he might have sealed up your cat in that outside wall over there. It weren't on purpose, you know. Shoot, J. W. loves cats. He's got a whole trailerful. Gray ones and black ones."

By this time, Mrs. Smith was hovering near a borderline stroke, but she managed to stammer out another question.

"How in George Washington's name did your man manage to do that?"

"J. W. says the cat was . . . Precious, you say his name was? Uh, Precious was curled up behind the insulation, and J. W. figures he must have fallen asleep. Now we can tear out the wall, but it's going to cost a little more. I didn't know how attached you were to the cat, uh, Precious, and all."

Fortunately, unlike some home remodeling tales, this

one has a happy ending. Mrs. Johnson found Precious in the neighbor's back yard with a female Persian before J. W. began tearing out the new wall. Mrs. Johnson's sister turned out to be allergic to cats, so now Precious is living in J. W.'s trailer, where he is constantly terrorized by J. W.'s four-year-old twins. And the new apartment? Mrs. Johnson's sister says it's wonderful, but some nights she swears she hears scratching noises. And the neighbors down the street still haven't found their missing orange cat.

Chapter 7

ROACHES AND REDNECKS

(A Low-Cost Guide to Pest Control)

EVEN THE CLEANEST house gets bugs once in a while. If it's termites—and you can tell pretty easily because part of your woodwork starts crumbling and there are all these flying ants around in the spring—you might as well call one of the leading exterminators and prepare to shell out four or five hundred dollars, depending on what part of the country you live in and what kind of car you have. BMW owners get a higher rate, as do those folks who drive Cadillacs or Mercedes. If you've got a '78 Chevy up on blocks and six kids with perennially runny noses, you might get them down to three hundred dollars.

Other household pests, with the possible exception of in-laws and grown children, can be controlled by the homeowner. The first thing you need to determine is what kind of insect problem you have. Somewhere during the evolutionary process, a bunch of the bugs got together and decided it would be best if they developed immunities against certain things. It would have been real simple if one thing, say DDT, wiped out all of the bugs. That way you wouldn't have to have several different types of sprays in your shed, depending on whether the bugs crawl, fly, chew leaves from the top or bottom, or go to Florida in the winter.

Unfortunately, a lot of the powerful insecticides also kill things they aren't supposed to, such as Junior's white mouse that he bought for that eighth-grade science experiment or all of your daughter's goldfish. It's kind of like warfare. Sure, George Bush could have used an atomic bomb on Saddam Hussein, but that would have been overkill. Instead, he dropped a couple of million smart bombs and launched a few thousand missiles that were programmed to hit only those soldiers with the astrological signs of Leo, Cancer, and Aquarius.

Unfortunately, you can't do that with pesticides. Each one has its own peculiarities, and each one requires appropriate action.

ROACHES

I suppose the most annoying pest is a cockroach. Cockroaches have been around since before Adam and they'll be here after we're gone. Like many of my relatives, they hole up during the day and come out only at night to eat. Left alone, cockroaches can spread disease and mess up books, clothes, and other things. Plus, they're unsightly. I was at a friend's house in the upscale part of town for a dinner party when one of the guests spotted a cockroach crawling across the kitchen counter. That may have been the only roach within miles, but it did the trick. My friend's wife was mortified, the guests lost their appetite, and the couple's reputation was shot.

The best thing to get rid of roaches is boric acid. You can buy products that contain boric acid at most hardware stores. Sprinkle it on plastic lids and leave it under cabinets or wherever you have a roach problem. Freshen it every week or so and before long you won't see a single roach. Trust me.

HOUSEFLIES

Houseflies are even worse than roaches. At least a roach simply crawls over your food; he doesn't fly around your head and light on your nose. There are a number of good aerosol sprays for houseflies, as well as fly bait that you can put outside. Just keep this away from pets and children.

Of course, you can always do what my Uncle Frank used to do and hang strips of flypaper all across the front and back porches. It didn't get rid of all the flies, but it sure thinned out the door-to-door salesmen.

MICE AND RATS

A mouse is one of those cute little cartoon creatures that are always outsmarting cats. A mouse is a mouse until it is seen by a woman; then it's a rat. This is one of those gender things I have never figured out. Somehow, when an ordinarily fearless woman who knows karate, judo, kung-fu, and other Oriental words sees a mouse, it is transformed in her mind into a foot-long vicious rodent. Usually the mouse is more frightened of us.

There are several ways of getting rid of mice, short

of getting several cats (and they bring in problems of their own):

- *Rat and Mice Bait.* This is a terrible thing that causes hemorrhaging and death. A few days later, you'll find these exploded bodies out near your faucet, and you'll feel really bad.
- *Mouse Traps.* These are the ones with the spring that you have to put a piece of cheese on (actually, peanut butter is better) and then set without getting your finger mashed. Then the next day you have to dispose of a mouse with a broken neck.
- *Sticky Mouse Traps.* These are wonderful if you have sticky mice. Seriously, these are flat pieces of cardboard with sticky stuff on them and a piece of bait in the middle. It's kind of like a Tar Baby for mice. Once the unsuspecting creature steps on this stuff, it can't get loose. The Lawson kids got hold of some of these and left them out in the barn and caught dozens of mice, which they proceeded to give to the cats without removing the sticky portion. Uncle Leonard said watching those cats try to get the sticky traps off their paws was funnier than feeding peanut butter to his beagle.
- *Humane Mouse Traps.* These are for tree-huggers, vegetarians, and other sensitive types. These traps don't harm mice. They don't catch them, either, most of the time; but if they do, the mouse stays inside all night, secure and safe from harm until it can be released in a natural environment where owls and hawks and snakes are waiting hungrily for their next meal.
- *Ants.* Diazinon works well, or if they're household ants,

spray with an aerosol. Better yet, just pack a picnic basket and leave it on the back porch of one of your most obnoxious neighbors. Every ant in the county will be there within minutes.

• *Silverfish.* These are the slender insects that you see occasionally in your basement or in your bathtub. They love to eat the glue or paste off wallpaper and books. Use a spray with lindane, chlordane, or malathion. And read the directions.

• *Redneck Relatives.* Of all household pests, these are the most stubborn and most difficult to get rid of. They arrive unexpectedly, usually when the weather turns cold (those cheap trailers are not very well insulated) or when your brother-in-law hurts his back and gets laid off for the fourteenth time. They travel in packs of six or eight and drive rusted-out Plymouths or brand-new Camaros. They eat voraciously and indiscriminately, although a few varieties have been known to reject broccoli.

Sprays, insecticides, and insults don't work very well with these pests since they have built up an immunity over the years. The only way to get rid of them is to use the same method employed for roaches (without the boric acid). Do not leave food out. Do not store food in the refrigerator. Do not keep bread or snacks in the pantry. And eat nothing but broccoli and water for three days. It works. Trust me.

Chapter 8

CLOGGED DRAINS AND LEAKY PIPES

(Why Marriages Fail)

HAVE YOU EVER WONDERED why marriages seemed to last longer in the old days? It's very simple. Plumbing. To be more specific, the lack of indoor plumbing. A recent study by some professor whose name I can't pronounce stated that the average American husband spends two years of his life unclogging drains, caulking bathtubs, dealing with septic tank problems, and leaving the toilet seat up.

I don't know who this professor interviewed, but I know he didn't get around to my Cousin Leroy. Leroy's hobby is plumbing. It would have been his profession, like it was his daddy's and his daddy's before him, but Leroy never has gotten the hang of this new PVC pipe. He has yet to understand the difference between a T-joint, an elbow, and male and female connectors. You can imagine how irritable his wife is. Other than a shallow gene pool, the

problem with Leroy is he's too proud to ask for help. Leona says they haven't been able to use the kitchen sink in six months; the commode in the guest bathroom is still in pieces on the back porch; and the one shower that still works mysteriously switches from warm to cold water every thirty-seven seconds.

A lot of men are like Leroy when it comes to plumbing. A clogged drain? No problem. A leaky pipe? No problem. For some reason, men have been led to believe they are capable of handling any plumbing problem.

"How complicated can it be?" Roy Bill asked the other weekend when Eleanor said the kitchen sink was draining too slow.

"If Elmo of Elmo and Sons Plumbers can do it, so can you," I said. Elmo makes Leroy look like the grand champion on "Jeopardy." "Come on. I'll drive you to Home Depot."

We were met by a courteous clerk wearing an apron. I was a little suspicious until I saw all the clerks were wearing aprons. Roy Bill explained he had a problem with his kitchen sink.

"Probably needs to have the trap cleaned out," the clerk said.

"Ain't set no traps under there," Roy Bill explained. "We use them rat pellets."

"No, sir," the clerk said, suppressing a smile, "I meant the grease trap."

"I knew that," Roy Bill said. "I was just testing you."

"You may want to get new pipes, and connectors," the clerk suggested. "How big is your pipe?"

"I beg your pardon?" Roy Bill asked, flustered.

"Roy Bill, I think he means the pipe under the sink," I said.

"'Bout that big," Roy Bill said, holding up his thumb and forefinger in an approximate circle.

The clerk shook his head. "Probably standard ¾". He pulled a complete set of prepackaged sink pipes out and handed them to Roy Bill. "This is for a standard T-type connection. Is that the configuration of your sink drain?"

"Looks close enough," Roy Bill said, and I agreed.

While we were there, we had to pick up some PVC cement, some joint putty, a larger wrench, and a leaf blower (it was on special). At the cash register, I picked up another utility knife, a first-aid kit, and a flashlight that floats.

All in all, we spent $198.47, and we hadn't even gotten the drain disconnected yet.

To make a long story short, we never did get the pipes hooked up correctly. Roy Bill bought more pipe, another hacksaw to cut the pipe, and a gas grill that was on sale. The second day without water in the kitchen, Eleanor put her foot down—squarely on Roy Bill's hand—and suggested he call Elmo. Now!

Two hours later, the sink was operational again, without a leak.

"How did he do that?" Roy Bill whispered as we watched Elmo write out the bill while moving his lips over each letter.

"I think it has something to do with the way he wears his pants," I said. "He's not that much smarter than you."

"That'll be $114.97, plus the parts," Elmo said. "Comes to $160. Woulda been a lot cheaper if I didn't have to clean up that mess that other plumber left."

Well, Roy Bill learned a valuable lesson, and I hope you have, too. The only plumbing repairs I suggest you try (if you're a hapless handyman) are emergency ones in which your family or pets are in imminent danger of drowning. In that case, go immediately to your shut-off valve (and you should find out where that is) and turn off the water.

CLOGGED DRAINS

Occasionally, it becomes necessary to remove some of the objects that have been flushed down a drain, such as marbles, paper towels, bobby pins, and the remnants of your hairline. First try the standard Drano or related products. If that doesn't work, fashion a one-foot section of wire coat hanger into a straight piece with a small hook on one end. This is effective in bathroom sinks where the culprit is a gob of hair.

If the offending drain is a bathtub or a toilet, use the plumber's friend (no, not Denise—I'm talking about the plunger here).

Augers or steel snakes can be rented and used to run through drainpipes to clean out an obstruction, but if things are that bad, you might as well call Elmo the Plumber.

COMMODES

Repairing a commode is really about as simple as removing a ruptured appendix. Have you ever looked inside those tanks? What's that rubber ball for? And where does that chain go? There are kits you can buy to replace the flushing mechanisms. These have easy-to-follow directions. Otherwise, call Elmo. But for goodness' sake, keep your wife and daughter out of the house unless Elmo's wearing suspenders.

Chapter 9

STICKY DRAWERS AND SAGGING DOORS

(Household Problems You Should Never Discuss in Public)

A LOT OF THE PROBLEMS homeowners have don't require a professional handyman. Some things are so simple even a hapless handyman can do them. Take sticky drawers, for instance. No, I'm not talking about the kind your white trash relatives are familiar with, I'm referring to the ones in your dresser. Have you ever noticed how stubborn those things are in damp weather? That's because the wood has swollen.

All you need to do is rub a little candle wax on the edges, and the drawer should slide in and out easily. Remove the drawer for this, and rub the wax on the guide strips and edges. If it still sticks, you may have to use sandpaper. Sand down the spots that look like they are sticking, and keep trying until everything works smoothly.

STICKING DOORS AND SQUEAKY HINGES

Yes, I know that sounds like a sixties rock group, but they are two of the more common problems found in houses, and two of the easiest to fix. If a door is sticking, check to make sure the hinges haven't gotten loose. Tighten the screws and try the door again. If the screws have worked loose and will not tighten properly, remove them and fill the holes with wooden plugs or even pieces of wooden matches. Apply a little glue, hammer flat, let dry, and reinsert the screws. Sometimes you may have to remove the door and sand it down a little, or else run a jack plane or a block plane along the top or bottom of the door, wherever the sticking is occurring.

STICKY WINDOWS

Nothing is more annoying than trying to open a window that's stuck, especially if you are in a hurry to get in or get out. Once again, a little candle wax or paraffin applied to the tracks of a double-hung window should help. If you have windows with a sash cord, squirt a few drops of oil on the pulley shafts. Windows that have swollen from moisture can be loosened by tapping with a hammer and a block of wood (that's to prevent scarring of the window sash). Sometimes a freshly painted window will stick. In that case, wedge a putty knife between the sash and the stop molding by tapping it with a hammer and twisting the blade slightly.

CREAKY CHAIRS AND WOBBLY TABLES

A loose rung is usually the culprit for a creaky or wobbly chair. Try applying glue with one of those hypodermic needle things that allow you to squirt it in small openings. If that's not possible, and you can do so without too much trouble, remove the rung, sand off the old glue, and reinsert with a fresh coat. Adding a little plastic wood or wrapping the rung with a fine thread and then coating with glue will tighten up a stubborn rung. Use a belt-clamp to hold the chair together while the glue sets.

For a wobbly table, the simplest thing to do is to install corner braces. These are available at hardware stores, or you can make your own with a triangular piece of wood that you drill ⅛″ holes in and then insert drywall screws long enough to secure the block to the inside of each corner. But metal braces are fine. Nobody but your mother-in-law is going to crawl under the table to inspect it.

REPAIRING CRACKS IN YOUR WALL

My friend Roy Bill got some firsthand experience at repairing cracks in his wall last year. Well, he watched me do it. All I did was take some drywall compound (assuming you have a drywall wall) and smooth it on with a putty knife. After it dried twenty-four hours, I sanded it, primed it with some white latex paint, and repainted the wall to match the others. How did Roy Bill get cracks in his wall? It's a long story.

Normally, Eleanor is an even-tempered woman, but occasionally Roy Bill will stretch her patience to the breaking point. Take last Christmas, for instance. For weeks, Eleanor had been hinting that she wanted a pink sweater that was on sale at Belk's and possibly a new pair of earrings. Roy Bill obviously had his mind on something else because he waited until the last minute on Christmas Eve and arrived just after Belk's and every other depart-

ment store had closed. The only thing that was open was Fred's Fur and Fin and Hardware Emporium.

Now Roy Bill is no fool. He knew he couldn't allow Eleanor to wake up on Christmas morning with nothing under the tree. So he bought her a self-oiling chain saw and a stuffed raccoon, paid extra for the special Mark Trail gift wrap, and headed happily for home.

About 9:00 A.M. on Christmas morning I got a call from Roy Bill, who seemed to be in some distress.

"You've got to come over, Bubba. I swear the woman's lost her mind."

"I'm sorry, Roy Bill. We must have a bad connection. I keep hearing this roaring noise in the background like static."

"That ain't no static," Roy Bill shouted. "That's Eleanor's Christmas present."

By the time I got there, Eleanor had demolished the stuffed raccoon, sawed the legs off Roy Bill's favorite coffee table, and carved the names of all her old boyfriends in the living room wall with the chain saw, which was lying on the kitchen floor still idling when I arrived. A visibly shaken Roy Bill explained that Eleanor had gone to her mother's in a snit.

"Did Eleanor do all this?" I asked, surveying the damage.

"Yep."

"I didn't even know she could crank a chain saw."

"I showed her. She sounded real calm when she asked me. I thought she liked it. See here," he said, getting up and walking over to the saw, "it's got this safety brake on here and a self-oiler. It's real light."

I picked up a raccoon tail from underneath the edge of the La-Z-Boy.

"I guess she didn't like this either."

"I don't think so," he said, switching off the saw. "Bubba?"

"Yes, Roy Bill?"

"How we going to get all those names out of the wall?"

"Drywall compound," I said. "I've got a spare bucket in the workshop."

A few hours later, Roy Bill was relieved. We had covered

over the names of Eleanor's seventeen boyfriends, along with certain descriptive passages, and I had vacuumed up the remnants of the raccoon while Roy Bill made a desperate plea for Joe Yancey to open his pawn shop. He bought a set of diamond earrings from a G.I. who had shipped out to the Persian Gulf, then wrapped them in some Christmas paper he found in the closet.

By the time the drywall compound had been sanded and painted, everything was back to normal at the Cole household. Well, almost back to normal. Roy Bill hasn't gotten much rest since Eleanor started sleeping with the chain saw beside the bed.

Chapter 10

WHERE WERE YOU WHEN THE LIGHTS WENT OUT?

(Short-Circuiting Electrical Problems)

IF YOU ARE GOING to be fooling with electricity, you had better learn a few basic rules.

First, don't touch any of those wires. Second, learn the electrician's secret handshake. You won't find instructions for this handshake in any how-to book because it is more closely guarded than even the Masons' passwords (Brick and mortar, sticks and stones, hand me the trowel, and pass it on) or the Carpenters' Code (how much wood would a woodchuck chuck if a woodchuck would chuck wood?). Pick up one of those joy buzzers that fit in the palm of your hand at a gag shop, and carry it with you when you go to buy materials at a hardware store. Pick out your amps and ohms and volts and wire and stuff like a regular customer, but just before the clerk totals up the bill, reach out and shake his hand with the joy buzzer hidden in your palm. He will instantly know that you are one of the Secret Brotherhood of Electricians and will automatically deduct 15 percent. Either that, or he'll call security. Not every hardware store clerk knows the secret electrician's handshake.

If there are no gag shops in your town or all of the joy buzzers have been sold out after the last union meeting, you can improvise by tickling the clerk's hand vigorously with your middle finger while saying, "Hummmmmmm!" He'll understand. Or else he'll call security.

Use the Masons' and Carpenters' codes when shopping for masonry or woodworking products. Sometimes it takes a while for the clerks to catch on, so you may have to wink broadly several times. And occasionally you'll run into a skeptic who is not convinced you are a true craftsman. He may test you by asking, "Are you a contractor?"

That's when you stare blankly at him without speaking for at least five minutes, and when he repeats the question, you say, "Ma'am (or Sir), we ran into some problems on this other job, but we'll be right out tomorrow. It shouldn't cost more than a couple of hundred dollars." If he doesn't believe you're a contractor after that, you might want to consider shopping at another hardware store.

Anyway, back to current affairs. Most of us are terrified of electricity, with good reason. It will shock you, it will make you vibrate all over (like Naomi's elongated portable massager for those tired facial muscles), and in some cases, it will kill you. They don't call it the electric chair for nothing.

But handled properly, electricity is no more dangerous

than a mother of five with PMS. The first thing you should do when there is an electrical failure is to check the fuse box. I'm sorry. That's the second thing you should do. The first thing is locating the fuse box. Most modern houses have circuit breakers, switches that flip off when a circuit overloads (this usually happens when Junior is practicing his electric guitar, Sissy is drying her hair, and Mama is trying to iron off the same outlet).

Simply unplug some of the appliances, if that seems to be the problem, and flip the switch back to on. If you have the old-fashioned fuses that have to be removed, pry the old one out with a screwdriver and replace it with the same size. You should have an assortment of replacement fuses on hand for emergencies.

Other problems common to American households are blown lightbulbs. These are usually reasonably simple to fix unless you are a college professor or commission salesman. In that case, you may have to seek professional help. The first step is to locate the faulty bulb. That is easily done by turning on all the other lights in the room. The one that doesn't come on is the one that needs replacing.

Test the bulb to see if it is warm to the touch. Warm is fine. Searing, flesh-burning hot is not. In that case, use a handkerchief or glove to unscrew the bulb. Do this counterclockwise, Lamar. From your right to your left. Now check the wattage and replace it with a similar one. Dispose of the old bulb, and you're in business.

Prevention is really the best thing to do to avoid electrical failure. Get a professional electrician to check your house wiring to see if it is aluminum or copper. If it's aluminum, go ahead and spend the money to get it replaced with copper. It's a lot safer.

Next, check all lamp and appliance cords to make sure they are not frayed. Those that are can be wrapped with electrical tape.

All outlets should have faceplates.

TV sets and other appliances should be positioned where they have breathing room, not jammed up against cabinets or walls.

Unplug countertop appliances when not in use.

Don't use electrical appliances in the bathtub, no matter how much you like hot toast in the morning.

Don't use extension cords in place of additional outlets. Adding another outlet is cheap compared to the cost of rebuilding your house.

Go easy on the Christmas lights. When small aircraft begin circling your front lawn, you may have overdone it.

Buy a voltage tester and a continuity tester. They are inexpensive, and they take the guesswork out of whether an outlet is "live" or not.

Even hapless handymen can perform simple electrical repairs if they follow instructions and cut off all the electricity at the switchbox. All the switches should be clearly marked for oven, stove, washer, dryer, water heater, etc., and should be tested. Don't take it for granted that the switches are properly labeled. Switch on the appliance or light that you are working on, and then flip switches until it goes off.

Most often, a hapless homeowner will not have to deal with electricity, but occasionally a spouse will suggest installing ceiling fans. When that happens, pretend to lose your hearing or begin wallowing on the ground as if you are having a seizure. Do anything—I repeat, anything—to keep from having to install a ceiling fan. Not that it's that complicated, of course. By following directions and having at least one other person to help you, you can probably install one in, say, the length of time it takes to play a baseball double-header.

Whatever you do, make sure you buy the proper fan for your ceiling height. Lamar put up two in his mobile home, but they weren't the ceiling-hugger types, so they extended about six inches lower than he intended. Now everytime Loretta invites her friends from the Cut and Run Style Shoppe over for a Lusty Lingerie and covered dish party in the middle of the summer, they all have to crawl around on their hands and knees to keep the tops of their beehives from being lopped off. Lamar says he's been around the world three times and been to fourteen county fairs and two buzzard festivals, and he ain't never seen anything worse than a half-dozen hefty women crawling around in rejects from Frederick's of Hollywood while eating Ruffles® and green onion dip.

Chapter 11

ARE YOU SURE VAN GOGH STARTED THIS WAY?

(Painting and Wallpapering Without Getting Plastered)

NO MATTER HOW NEW your house is, sooner or later something is going to need painting or wallpapering. Maybe it's Junior's room after he got out of high school and decided that black and orange was not the proper color scheme for a college student. Or maybe it's the spare bedroom that you need for a nursery. I don't know if it's hormones or what, but the impending arrival of a baby turns ordinarily sane women into fanatic interior designers. Right after Eleanor broke the news to Roy Bill that her home pregnancy test came out positive, she started thumbing through wallpaper catalogs, looking at designs with little cherubs and ponies and flowers.

"And of course we'll need to paint the guest bathroom,

too," she said, dipping a dill pickle in a cup of Cool Whip.

"Why is that, hon?" Roy Bill asked innocently. "It looks fine the way it is now."

"But it's green, darling. You know Mother hates green."

"It's not her bathroom."

"Oh, but it will be hers for a few weeks after the baby comes. I'll need her to help out around the house."

"I can help out," Roy Bill said, his voice just one octave short of a whine. "I can cook and wash dishes and change diapers."

"Don't be silly, dear. You know mothers always come and live with their daughters when a baby is born."

Roy Bill knew that and I knew that. What we didn't know is *why?* I mean, Eleanor is a career woman who handles million-dollar transactions with one hand while she runs the household with the other. She has meals planned for the next six months. Probably has half of them already frozen and ready to microwave. But she and every other woman I know suddenly become helpless after their babies are born and need their mothers.

I asked Eleanor about this while Roy Bill was rummaging through his work shed trying to find a paintbrush that wasn't as stiff as Zachary Taylor.

"It's a tradition," she explained. "It creates a bonding between the generations."

"Kind of like Superglue?" I asked.

"No," she laughed. "Not that kind of bonding. A psychological bonding. It's something women have done since prehistoric times."

"What do men do?"

"They fall to pieces, usually," she said. "That's why we have to find things for them to do to take their minds off the birth process. Like painting and wallpapering and putting up new curtains."

"I thought all that was needed."

"Some of it. Sure, you need new curtains and baby furniture, but I really didn't need the bathroom repainted, and I didn't need to wallpaper the nursery. We could have gotten by with just a fresh coat of paint. But this way, see, Roy Bill will be so wrapped up in this project for the next three or four weekends, he won't have time to get nervous about the baby."

Well, Eleanor was right. Roy Bill was a total wreck for the next month. After spending a day with him buying new paintbrushes, paint, masking tape, and mineral spirits, I was called in as a neutral third party to help pick out the wallpaper.

I immediately chose the one with toy soldiers.

"Too militaristic," Eleanor said. "Besides, what if it's a girl?"

"Girls like soldiers," I said. "At least my Aunt Nona did. She spent so much time at Fort Jackson, they gave her a sticker for her Jeep."

"I didn't know your Aunt Nona was in the army." Eleanor said.

"She wasn't. She was a civilian volunteer in charge of boosting morale. There was a whole group of women like her. They wore black fishnet stockings and carried beaded bags."

"I like the wallpaper with the bluebirds and cherubs," Eleanor said, changing the subject.

"Too sissified," Roy Bill said. "What if it's a boy?"

"Why don't you use alternating strips of the toy soldiers and the cherubs," I suggested.

"Too confusing," they both said. "The poor child won't have a clue as to its sexual identity."

They eventually settled on a nice blue-and-pink pattern with bunnies and kittens and other furry creatures frolicking in a meadow. A wise choice, I thought. And the easiest. The rest of the process was all downhill. Roy Bill and I made complete fools out of ourselves over the next few weekends, covered up windows and wall outlets and a sleeping cat in the process, and got more paste on the woodwork than we did on the walls. Finally, Roy Bill found a business card at Kroger's listing a woman who hung wallpaper for reasonable rates. He hired her in secret, sent Eleanor and her mother to the mall with thirty-seven dollars and a Rich's card, and called in the professional to put up the paper.

Everything looked wonderful by the time Eleanor and her mother, Eufala, returned. Eleanor bubbled with praise for Roy Bill's skill, but Eufala just wandered around looking at the walls, sucking on a Kool that never left the corner of her mouth, muttering, "There's something fishy going on here. This boy couldn't pour beer out of a boot with the instructions on the heel. I know he can't hang wallpaper this good."

Well, if you are lucky enough to find a professional wallpaper hanger who will do the job for less than the price of a compact car, hire him or her immediately. It's up to you if you want to deceive your wife or husband. Otherwise, I advise avoiding hanging wallpaper like you would avoid your freeloading brother-in-law. In fact, your brother-in-law would stick around a lot longer than any wallpaper you put up yourself.

If your wife insists on something other than a nice coat of paint, talk her into using one of those six-inch borders of wallpaper or stenciling around the top of the walls near the ceiling. It looks very nice and is not nearly as much trouble as putting up entire sheets of wallpaper.

PAINTING

If you have never painted before, this is a job that is almost as enjoyable as desexing lambs on an Australian sheep farm. Before you start, you will need to have several important items:

- A blender. No, this is not for the paint. This is to mix the daiquiris you will need before the job is finished.
- Paintbrushes. There are several kinds of paintbrushes: those that are too wide, those that are too narrow, those with loose bristles, and those that cost more than a registered cocker spaniel. No matter what kind you get, it will be the wrong kind; so get an assortment of one-, two-, three-, and six-inch brushes. You might as well buy a good quality brush if you have a lot of painting to do, but if you're like Roy Bill and never remember to clean it from one job to the next, an economy model will probably do just as well.
- Rollers and paint trays and spare buckets.
- Paint sprayer—if you are painting an exterior and your house is quite large. Rent this from a tool rental place, unless your neighbor or father-in-law has one.
- Stepladder, step stool, and extension ladder, depending on how high you have to paint. I always make it a rule never to climb higher than Refrigerator Perry can jump. If you have a lot of two-story outside painting, you might want to consider renting some scaffolds or hiring somebody else to do the work.
- Masking tape for baseboards, moldings, and windows.
- A stocking mask and a crowbar (I'm sorry. Ignore that.

I was looking at my cousin Moonlight Mulligan's tool list by mistake).

- Drop cloths (Even Michelangelo used these in the Sistine Chapel; it's hell painting those ceilings without spilling a few drops).
- A big Hefty garbage bag. Cut out holes for your head and arms and put it over you. This keeps any paint you spill from getting on your clothes. Just remember to take it off before you go out in public, or you might be mistaken for one of the guys from the Fruit-of-the-Loom commercial.
- The paint. Latex is good for almost all jobs now, and it cleans up with soap and water.

Before you start, get your son and his friends to take the furniture out of the room, put down drop cloths around the edges, and mask all the woodwork with tape. If you can get him to do that, you are more persuasive than I am.

Fill in any holes or imperfections a day or two earlier and sand smooth. Take down all curtain rods and hardware and remove electrical outlet faceplates.

If you are using a roller, use mohair or synthetic fibers. They don't mat as easily as lamb's wool and can be used on most surfaces. If the surface is smooth, you can use a shorter nap (on the roller; we're not talking about sleep here). Use an extension handle, and you won't have to keep climbing up on stools to paint near the ceiling. After going over the walls with one coat, touch up the edges with a brush, let dry for a few hours, then apply a second coat. Be patient and careful, and you won't have to spend half a day cleaning up.

If you are painting outside, make sure you have lots of insurance and no holly bushes directly beneath the ladder, which should be positioned with both legs on the ground and at an angle that is not too steep.

Of course, if you truly want to avoid ever doing this kind of work again, you could do like my Cousin Luther, who pretended to fall off a ladder from the second story of his house and hurt his arm so his wife would take pity on him. He would have gotten away with it, too, if Lavinia hadn't seen him bowling the next night with Debbie Ann from the Dairy Swirl. Do you know how long it takes to paint a house with a half-inch trim brush? Just ask Luther. It's been three years now, and he's not finished yet.

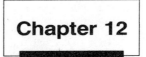

Chapter 12

HITTING THE ROOF

(What to Do to Keep Mother Nature from Coming Inside)

NEW ROOFS with the asphalt and Fiberglas shingles are reasonably efficient, but they just don't have the charm of a tin roof. When I was growing up, we had a tin roof and very little insulation. Make that no insulation. I lived in a one-hundred-year-old farmhouse made of weathered pine. During very heavy rainstorms, the roof leaked on the side porch and occasionally in the hallway. Mama took care of the problem by putting dishpans or foot tubs under the leak. The next day, providing the rain had stopped and everything had dried out, my father would climb on the roof with a bucket of tar and patch any holes where the nails had worked loose.

A few leaks were a small price to pay for the pleasure of going to sleep with the sound of raindrops on the tin roof. Depending on the intensity of the rain, the sounds ranged from a soft lullaby to a Wagner opera. It was the best feeling in the world because you were separated from nature by only a thin sheet of metal.

Like most country folks, my father couldn't wait to get rid of the tin and put down a layer of plywood and real shingles. Shortly after that, he put in new windows and insulation, replaced the weathered, unpainted siding with new wood, and painted it two coats of a grayish-green.

"Now you have a modern-looking house," my friend E. L. said. "You must be proud."

I was proud. Too proud, I realize now. While it's true that insulation and roofing are energy efficient (that's the buzz word for the nineties), they don't have the romance of the old tin roofs and drafty siding. Of course, neither does Christmas, but that's another story.

If you have a modern roof and you live in the house for more than ten or twelve years, sooner or later you will notice signs of deterioration followed by an annoying leak when the wind blows during a heavy rainstorm. Now is the time to take action. Immediately put your house on the market and try to sell it before the next thunderstorm. If that's impractical, prepare to spot the source of the leak and patch it by replacing worn shingles with new ones and gluing them down with a roofing cement. Leaks usually occur at flashings (around your chimney or gas vent pipes), in valleys, or at the eaves. The best time to spot a leak is when it's raining. No, this doesn't require you to go outside. Simply go into the attic, crawl over the fourteen boxes of baby clothes your wife refuses to throw away, step over the boxes of Christmas wrapping paper and ornaments, make your way through the piles of old stuffed animals and board games, and see where the moisture is accumulating on the underside of the roof.

Drive a nail through the roof so you can find the hole when you get on the roof. Later, when the sun is shining, go onto the roof and see if you can spot the cause of the problem, other than the nail sticking through. Is the wood soft underneath the shingles? If it is, you may have to replace that section of plywood and add another layer of roofing felt and another layer of shingles. If you're lucky, all that will be wrong is that a shingle will have come loose and needs to be glued down or replaced.

To replace a damaged shingle, lift up the tab on the shingle covering it and remove the nails using a crowbar on a flat nail-puller. Pull out the old shingle and check the roofing felt to make sure it is still good. Hold the flap up on the shingle above it, and nail the new shingle into place.

If the leak is around your chimney flashing, try caulking all around it with some of the new silicone caulking that expands with the weather. Small holes or cracks in shingles can be repaired with roofing cement. If the shingle is torn, use a putty knife to spread a layer of roofing cement under the tear. If necessary, nail each side in place with roofing nails.

That about takes care of any roofing problems, short of replacing the entire roof. When that becomes necessary, don't, I repeat, *don't* attempt it yourself. It is worth whatever the roofing contractor charges you to remove the old shingles, haul them away, and replace them with new twenty-five-year shingles that will last about ten years.

Or you could go back to tin and explain to your wife you're doing it for the romance. If she believes that, tell her you're getting a new bass boat so you can take her on moonlight cruises on Clarks Hill Reservoir. It worked for Curtis LaGrone. Well, sort of. May Bell LaGrone is what you might call a full-bodied woman. She buys all her clothes at Ramona's Big Girl Barn and has ruined more car springs than all of the engineers at the General Motors testing center. She is to the Dairy Swirl what Tammy Faye Bakker is to Revlon.

Anyway, May Bell thought that bass boat was the most romantic thing Curtis had ever done, except for ripping off those old asphalt shingles and replacing them with shiny new sheets of tin. From then on, every time Curtis mentioned a fishing trip, May Bell got ready to go. This would have lasted indefinitely, I guess, if she hadn't gone with him to check trotlines one night. I suppose an eel does look something like a water moccasin when you're as excitable as May Bell. Curtis always carried a little .410 shotgun with him in case he saw a snake, but I guess he had no idea May Bell knew how to use it. Kelly Wayne about has all of those holes patched up in the boat, but it's going to take a little longer to salvage that 125-hp Evinrude. About as long as it's going to take for Curtis to regain his pride after the boys at the Gulf—I mean BP— station heard about what happened.

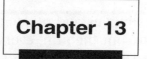
WHERE THE BOYS ARE

(A Woman's Guide to Hardware Stores)

WITH THE INVENTION of building supply warehouses like Home Depot, which feature lighting and decorating items as well as everything else, and the chain hardware stores, which are a lot more sanitary than the old-fashioned neighborhood stores, women have started turning out in droves to buy tools and things for the house and garden.

Initially, women began going to building supply stores because their husbands always forgot what they went there for in the first place. Poor Lorena Newhouse has been trying to get Herb to bring her a pair of gardening gloves and some tomato fertilizer for two weekends. Herb returned on Saturday with a new set of wrenches and a rubber-coated flashlight that doubled as a billy club. The next weekend he came back with four screwdrivers, a rotisserie attachment for the gas grill, and a case of light bulbs.

"Where are my gloves and my fertilizer?" Lorena asked in a tone of voice that made all the dogs in the neighborhood start howling.

"I guess I forgot," Herb said sheepishly while he unscrewed the flashlight to insert new batteries.

"Never mind," Lorena snapped. "I'll go myself."

"Uh, honey, you'd better not do that. Those places are dangerous with all those tools and boxes up on the shelves and those strange men wandering around. I'll go back."

"No, you won't," Lorena said, fishing the keys to the truck out of her purse. "I'll be curious to find out what's so interesting about these places anyway."

What Lorena saw was a real eye-opener. Her impression of hardware stores was from the days when her daddy used to take her to town to buy a new saw or a blade for his axe. These stores were musty and dark as a dungeon and about as thoughtfully laid out. Usually there were three or four farmers standing around, seeing who could spit tobacco juice closest to a mark on the floor. No customer could walk in and find what he was looking for. The owner of the store or his hired hand had to be summoned and the desired part or tool described; then the customer had to wait twenty minutes while a boy wearing overalls and a crew cut crawled over old boxes and eventually found what was needed.

It was real homey, but kind of scary to women who were used to clean, well-lighted aisles in the Piggly-Wiggly or Ramona's Dress Barn.

That's why Lorena was pleasantly surprised when she went into the new building supply warehouse. Sure, it's a little intimidating at first because there is all this *stuff* piled up on shelves and stacked in the aisles. But after a while Lorena learned to read the signs hanging at the end of each aisle for hardware, plumbing, electrical, tile, gardening, and so forth. It was just like being in Kmart. There were even shopping carts for her convenience.

She found the gloves and the fertilizer and a nice flat of marigolds and tomato plants in the garden shop. The next weekend, she called Wynona to go with her and look for some new indoor/outdoor carpet for the porch. Now they go there every week. It's like a little outing.

Lorena and Wynona discovered what men have known all along. Hardware stores are addictive. Well, maybe it's not as bad for women as it is for men. But few of us can walk into a hardware store or a Home Depot without leaving with a sackful of impulse purchases. Everything is so handy and so useful and so *necessary*. Besides, we tell ourselves, since it's for the house, it's really an investment. It's not personal. Sure, I bought that radial arm saw and the lathe, but that was to do home improvements. It wasn't for me.

And that's another difference between women and men. Give a woman a new blender or a curly-fry potato peeler for her anniversary, and she gets mad enough to chew nails. Or else she starts crying, which is worse.

"What's wrong, honey?" you ask, genuinely bewildered.

"It's, it's so . . . *practical!*" she sobs. "Couldn't you have gotten me something I *didn't* need?"

No wonder men have started painting their faces and going out in the woods to sit around a campfire and beat their tom-toms. You see, men *love* practical things. No man is offended if he is given a new saw or a hammer or some woodworking gadget. Even if it is a tool that is re-

quired for a complex, dirty, unfulfilling home improve-ment project, he is happy to get it.

"Of course," you women are saying now, "he's a man. He's supposed to like tools." Yes, that's true. But he prob-ably would like a fishing rod or some new lures or a new semiautomatic shotgun that he could take into the woods to stalk the fearsome quail and the deadly rabbit. Men assume that if something is practical, it is a wonderful gift.

Women, on the other hand, delight in getting filmy underwear that wouldn't stand up to a stiff breeze without tearing. They love getting little trinkets and stuffed animals and big trinkets and coats made from small furry animals.

That's why women like the new hardware stores and men prefer the old ones. Well, let me backtrack a little. Men like the new stores and the super warehouses if they're actually going there to buy something they need. But if they're going out to hang around with other men and catch up on the local gossip, they head straight for the dirtiest, most cluttered hardware store they can find. On the way they stop at a 7-Eleven and get some Red Man chewing tobacco.

The old-fashioned hardware store is the last bastion of maleness. It is a wonderful place where sweaty farmers and Irish Spring-smelling lawyers can mingle with one goal in mind: to stay out of the house until their mothers-in-law leave, their children go off to college, their wives get in a better mood, or the Braves doubleheader begins, whichever comes first. While they're there, they might browse around in the tool section or check the china pattern of the couples who are about to get married. That's right. In small towns, hardware stores put the china patterns up front so the women can inspect the dishes without having to venture too far into the bowels of the store where the cotter pins, hognose rings, and other exotic items are kept.

But mainly the men stand around, spit, trim their fingernails with pocketknives, swap tall tales and gossip, and pretend they're in total control of their households and their destinies. The sad part is, many are not even in total control of their bodily functions, which is another reason women don't go into those kinds of stores.

If, however, you are a woman and you are forced to buy something at one of the nonchain stores where there are no helpful hardware men, follow these simple rules:

- Don't wear sandals or other open-toed shoes.
- Avoid sundresses or anything that shows a lot of skin.
- Always wear a bra. Two, if possible. The last time Betty Lou Bradshaw went braless into Willett's Hardware, they had to call the emergency medical service for Jethro Plum and Wallace Whitman. Jethro did have a mild coronary, but Wallace just got strangled when a mouthful of tobacco juice went down his windpipe.
- Don't wear makeup. I know you look better, but some of those old goats are just waiting for the slightest bit of encouragement.
- Don't tell them you are a recent widow or divorcée unless you have a fire hose at your house that you can spray on the predators that will show up to "help you with some nighttime chores."
- Jogging suits are permissible, as long as you have strips of reflective tape on them. Those stores are pretty dark, and it'll help the clerks locate you if you wander down the wrong aisle.
- Don't wander down the wrong aisle. Not even the owners of these stores know what's in some of those rooms. Ralph Lawson found six-gallon jars filled with pickled rattlesnakes in the back of the Modoc Hard-

ware Store, apparently left over from the previous owner.

- Act confident. Old men like that in a woman. It shows spunk.
- Under no circumstances should you know the exact name and size of the item you need. The best approach is to giggle and say, "I don't know what you call it, but it fits on the end of this long thing that goes in the back of the lawn mower." And six men will immediately identify the part as a ⅝-inch hexagonal double-jointed wing nut with a triple-coated lock washer.
- Pay in cash. If the store accepts credit cards, it will take the clerk a good half-hour to find the forms and dust them off.
- If you are buying a large, heavy item, don't attempt to put it in your car yourself. They will gladly load it for you. In fact, if you are an attractive woman under seventy-four, they will tote it on their backs and deliver it within a five-mile radius.
- Don't tip. The best thing you can do is lightly pat them on the forearm and compliment them on their strength.
- And don't make wisecracks, such as, "Well, yes, I really get turned on by men who don't bathe and still have three of their adult incisors." It may work on "Roseanne," but it won't fly at the Happy Valley Hardware Store.

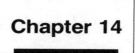
THE BLUFFER'S GUIDE FOR HAPLESS HANDYMEN

(How to Look and Act Like a Professional Even If You Don't Know a Ratchet from a Hatchet)

EVEN IF YOU CAN'T be a competent handyman, there's no reason to let anyone outside of your immediate family know it. If you dress like you know what you're doing, talk like you know what you're doing, and act like you know what you're doing, people will automatically *believe* you know what you're doing. Look at Ronald Reagan. A majority of voters *still* believe he knew what he was doing simply because he looked like a president and acted like a president.

One word of warning here: You don't want to be *too* convincing, or else some of your neighbors will start asking you to help them install disappearing stairways or attic fans. Whenever that occurs, shake your head slowly and express your regrets sincerely.

"I'd like to help you, Fred, but Gladys has so many projects lined up I've been busier than a set of jumper cables at a redneck funeral." That ought to stall him for a while, and by then you can think of another excuse.

DRESSING THE PART

I cannot overstress the importance of appearance when it comes to handymen or anything else. One reason I was never a successful hunter is that I never had the proper clothes. While my Uncle Jim was putting on his insulated underwear, camouflage pants and shirt, ammunition vest, wool socks, and insulated boots, I was pulling on a pair of blue jeans, a red flannel shirt, and a pair of high-top PF Flyers. While Uncle Jim had enough guns to keep Pancho Villa in business for weeks, I was forced to use a single-shot .22 rifle that misfired about as often as it shot.

If you're going to pass yourself off as a knowledgeable handyman, you have to look like one. You will need several outfits, depending on whether you are painting, carpentering, plumbing, bricklaying, or electricianing.

Painters. Always wear white overalls and painters' caps and brogans that are splattered with various shades of latex and oil-based tints. If you are just starting out, and have never painted, you need to put on a set of clean clothes, stand in the back yard away from the patio furniture, and have your wife fling paint on you. A couple of hours of this should be enough. And don't use only one color; the experts can see right through that trick.

Acting like a painter requires a certain skill. If you are visiting someone else's house, walk around slowly run-

ning your fingers along the wall and shaking your head. Occasionally mumble, "One coat" or "Too much thinner." Carry a batch of paint-chip samples in your pockets at all times, and at the appropriate moment, whip them out and say, "You know, Edna, this seafoam aquamarine would really complement those peach draperies over there. If I weren't so tied up for the next eighteen months, I'd offer to do the job myself. But I'm sure your husband doesn't have anything planned during the weekend of the Super Bowl."

Carpenters. Once again, a good pair of overalls with a rule pocket and a hammer loop on the side is essential. And *don't* get the cutesy designer kind, no matter how much your wife insists. Go to a small-town general store and wander all the way to the back, past the khaki work trousers, until you see the stacks of overalls. Buy the correct size and wash it in a weak mixture of bleach for about four days. In between washings, take the garment outside, lay it on the driveway, and run over it with the truck several times.

Immediately saw some boards so you can get sawdust to sprinkle in your hair and in your pockets. Work up a good sweat and add more sawdust. Put a used folding rule in your side pocket and a battered hammer in the loop, a couple of pencils in your bib pencil holder, and a handful of nails in your left pocket; pour a generous helping of RC Cola on your right pants leg and you're almost ready to pass for an expert carpenter.

I said *almost.* There's one little thing, and this is the step that separates the journeymen from the apprentices, the cabinet makers from the nail drivers. I want you to hit your thumb with your hammer hard enough to make the nail turn blue. Now I have known some men so squeamish they have actually *painted* their thumbnails with some of their wife's purple nail polish. Sure, it looks passable in dim light, but if you're standing out on the back deck with some of the boys from Hewatt's Hardware, they're going to take one look at your thumb and make a joke about your tendency to use women's makeup.

"Next thing you know, he's going to be wearing one of them corsets," J. T. will say, and they'll all laugh. You'll never be able to go into the hardware store on Saturday morning without enduring endless jokes.

But it's your choice. You can cheat, or you can hammer away.

Acting like a carpenter requires a lot of humming to yourself when you're visiting a new house that a friend has just bought with all of his life savings and is having difficulty meeting the mortgage payments. He's naturally proud of his new home, but most carpenters cannot leave well enough alone. I know. My father was a carpenter. He never walked into a house that he didn't find something wrong within five minutes.

"Look here. They messed up on the molding and tried to hide it with plastic wood. And see that doorjamb there? It must be three-sixteenths out of plumb."

I, of course, never could see any of those things, which is why I bought a house that started falling down right after I got the curtains hung. You don't have to see any of these things either. You just have to be convincing in pointing them out.

Say things like, "What kind of vapor barriers have you got, Art?" And when the poor guy says he doesn't know, just nod wisely. Or say, "Art, I was noticing you don't have continuous roof vents. I guess you don't mind replacing your shingles in a couple of years." Just make sure that the guy you're telling this to is as hapless as you are. And that's easy. Just follow my guide from Chapter 3 about how to spot a hapless handyman. If this sucker's wearing a pair of scuffed Weejuns and owns a Kmart hammer, casually ask, "Art, does your wife still have her dado?" And that ought to prove it once and for all.

Plumbers. No special clothes are needed for plumbing; any kind of green or khaki work pants will do. Buy them a size too big, wear them over hip-hugger briefs, and crawl around under your house (assuming you have a crawl space) one Saturday morning until you have wiped up most of the debris and cobwebs. Now fill your pockets with some galvanized pipe fittings, a small pipe wrench, and a large pipe wrench and practice getting down on your hands and knees and looking under the kitchen sink. This position is crucial, for if your pants do not slide down over the crack of your rear end, you are doing something wrong. Try adding more pipe fittings. If that doesn't work, you're going to have to go back and get another size larger and plan on spending yet another morning crawling around under the house.

Acting like a plumber means you'll have to crawl around under the house a lot and inspect the pipes. Let your pants sag. Learn the vocabulary. Casually mention to your neighbor's wife that you'll be glad to check her plenum before it gets too cold; and if she has an afternoon free, you'll be happy to make sure her escutcheon is still tight. It would also help to know what these terms mean in case she asks.

Bricklayers. This is an easy one. Wear basically the same kind of clothes as a carpenter or plumber, but make sure they fit. Bricklayers are the fashion plates of blue-collar workers. You will, however, need a good pair of steel-toed work shoes and the ability to tolerate weeks of dry skin from handling concrete and masonry products. Having a layer of mortar under your fingernails will add to the authentic look.

Acting like a bricklayer means you should check the joints between bricks at your friends' houses frequently and ask if they know how safe their chimney is. Know all four verses to "Nobody Knows My Trowels." Repeat the Masons' secret code a lot, but not too loudly. Know several kinds of bricks, and be able to identify them on sight. Carry a brick mason's hammer with you, and chip off a little piece of brick from your neighbor's back wall, hold it up to the light, and announce that it was made from clay mined three miles outside of Birmingham in 1987. If they buy that, then offer to sell them your 1976 Buick Skylark with "just under 37,000 miles. It's as solid as a brick."

Electricians. Wear plumbers' clothes. Loose-fitting pants are essential, but instead of filling your pockets with pipe fittings, hang a tool belt around your waist with an assortment of screwdrivers, splicing pliers, and needlenose pliers. Practice squatting in front of an electrical outlet until your pants have crept down to a revealing point. Rubber-soled shoes are advisable.

Acting like an electrician begins by learning to be real jumpy during thunderstorms. Refuse to plug in any appliance—even the toaster—until you have pulled out your outlet tester (don't do this in front of young children). Always carry a pocketful of amps and ohms and volts to hand out as party favors. Kids love them.

Chapter 15

INSTALLING PANELING WITHOUT CLIMBING THE WALLS

(How to Spend a Fortune Making the Inside of Your Home Look Cheap)

EVERYONE, I'M SURE, has been inside an elegant home that was beautifully constructed with fine moldings and rich, dark paneling that was reminiscent of a fine English gentleman's club. Or perhaps some of you are old enough to remember knotty pine paneling, that decorating craze that swept the nation back in the 1950s along with lime green Fiberglas drapes and Danish modern furniture.

Now don't get me wrong; I like knotty pine paneling fine, as long as it's used in moderation in one room of the house, say, the family room or the den, or even the kitchen. But it makes me kind of claustrophobic to see knotty pine paneling *everywhere,* even on the ceilings. Some people have gotten carried away and turned their otherwise nice homes into something that resembled the Soap Creek Sportsman Lodge and All-You-Can-Eat Catfish Cafe.

As for lime green drapes and Danish modern furniture, I'm about as fond of that as I am Richard Simmons' wardrobe. But everybody to his own taste, as Abijean Montrose said right after her husband Morton ran off with the male assistant manager of the Putt-Putt. "At least they can wear each other's clothes," said Abijean, who always shopped with Morton in the big-and-tall section of Kmart.

But times have changed, as Abijean says, and knotty pine paneling is now considered "quaint" or "retro." Today's paneling is more subdued in tone and a lot easier to install than knotty pine.

There are three types of paneling for the do-it-yourselfer:

Hardwood/Plywood. These sheets have impressive finishes in oak, birch, pecan, or whatever. They look and feel like real wood because, on the surface at least, they are. You can't afford this, so you might as well go to the next type.

Plywood Paneling. This is made from thin layers of wood glued together with a prefinished veneer or natural finish. This is a little less expensive than the hardwood/plywood, and if your wife's working, you might be able to afford this.

Cardboard Paneling. Actually, I don't know what this paneling is made of. Sawdust, I think, or something synthetic. There are different grades, of course. The cheaper quality warps after the first hot day or thunderstorm; more expensive grades will not warp until the day before your finicky in-laws arrive for a week's visit and you sud-

denly notice that your walls look like the surface of the
Brown Sea. If you are like most of us hapless handymen,
this is the kind of paneling you will buy, simply because
you can save a few bucks. Never mind that it's going to
cost you an arm and a leg later to rip out the cheap stuff
and install a better grade of paneling. Yes, I know you plan

on fixing up the house and selling it next week, so you don't want to sink a lot of money into expensive materials, but isn't that what you said when you used the untreated wood on the deck that you had to replace last year? Never mind. It's your money.

WHAT YOU'LL NEED

You probably have the tools you need for a paneling job right next door in your neighbor's workshop. Before borrowing them, however, make sure that he has sharpened all the saws recently. If not, you might suggest that he replace the blade on his power saw with one that is suitable for cutting paneling. A combination hollow-ground blade is good. If you use a table saw, keep the face of the paneling up; with a handsaw or portable power saw, keep the face down. Always use masking tape along the line to be cut to avoid splintering.

You will also need a power drill with at least a ½-inch wood drill bit and a jigsaw or saber saw with the appropriate blade for cutting paneling. Other things you'll probably need are a nailset, a good hammer, a rubber mallet, a wood chisel, a plumb bob, a block plane, and a compass—one you use to draw circles (your kids should have one in their school supply box).

If you're paneling a new room, such as a basement addition, you've got it made. There are no moldings to take down, nothing to move. And if you're using a thicker type of paneling, there is no need to add furring strips. Check the surface of the studs (those are the straight up and down 2 x 4s) to make sure they are even. Use a block plane to smooth out any high spots and shims (thin strips of wood that you can buy at a building supply store) to even out the low spots. Install a vapor barrier with plastic sheeting or building paper against the outside wall to protect from moisture.

Most of us, however, will be installing paneling in rooms that already have something on the walls. Either cheap paneling or drywall. In this case, you will probably need a stud finder (No, Lamar, not Yolande Gilbert. She's a different kind of stud finder). This is a device that you can use to locate the studs (it picks up on where the nails are) so you will not end up trying to nail a panel into a hollow spot on the wall. Normally, studs are set every sixteen inches on center, but some builders cut corners and put them every twenty-four inches. And if your house is very old, there's no telling what measurements they used.

If your walls are smooth and even, you can install the paneling directly over them. An easy way to check is by holding a room-length piece of straight 2 x 4 against the wall. If the board is flush, then the wall is even. Check in several places, both horizontally and vertically. Uneven walls can be taken care of by using furring strips, or 1 x 2 or 1 x 3 strips of wood. Nail these strips 16 inches apart, either horizontally or vertically. Put extra strips around doors and windows, and use shims to even out low spots.

To install, start in the corner and work your way out. Use color-coated paneling nails that match the paneling. Paneling adhesive applied to the old wall or the furring strips will guard against buckling along the edges. By measuring exactly, you should be able to locate where the outlet boxes and electrical switches will fall on the new paneling. Mark the appropriate area on the panel, drill four holes at each corner, put masking tape around it, and use a jigsaw to cut out the opening.

Another method is to rub chalk around the edges of electrical outlets (you should have the face plates off, of course) and place a piece of paneling against that wall. Use a rubber mallet to tap firmly against the spot where the outlet is. That will leave a chalk outline on the back of the panel, which you can use to cut the opening.

If you're a beginner, obviously you will make a few mistakes. Don't despair. Most paneling cracks or scars can be filled in with colored sticks available at your hardware store, and the larger ones along the bottom can be disguised by placing sofas or chairs in front of them. For the imperfections around eye level, simply hang a work of art. There is nothing like a few velvet paintings of Elvis and bullfight scenes to distract a visitor's eye from the shoddy job you did on the paneling.

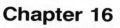

Chapter 16

JUST ASK BUBBA

(Stupid Questions from Confused Homeowners)

I REALIZE THIS BOOK does not cover all aspects of home improvements, so I have included a sampling of the most-asked questions. Now as you read some of these, I am sure you are going to say, "Golly, Bubba, these people sure are dumb." Yes, I know, but you must bear in mind that many of these questions come from nonprofessionals, such as commission salesmen, politicians, astrophysicists, and women who watch daytime television too much, so what do you expect? Anyway, there may be a few gems among this selection that will enlighten even the most callused handyman.

Dear Bubba:
  Why is it that even very smart women are so afraid of anything mechanical?
                    Wondering Widow in Wisconsin

Dear Wondering:

That's a very good question. It's true that many of the women I have met have difficulty dealing with mechanical things, unless it's an automatic teller machine. I think this has something to do with their genes, which usually are worn too tight. More likely, it's because they are smarter than most men and know better than to get their hands

greasy and break their nails on stuff they can get men to fix just by batting their eyelashes a couple of times. Besides, men are so easily intimidated by women who can do things better than they can. I have known women who rebuild Suzuki transmissions all day but who ask their husbands to tighten the screws on the TV antenna. Another reason is that women are too analytical. They want to know why a carburetor does what it does, just as they want to know why a relationship is or isn't working. Men just stick the parts in without questions. "Why'd you put that doohickey there?" you can ask Monroe, and Monroe will say, "Because Earl told me to."

Dear Bubba:

If the clock on my VCR keeps flashing 9:45 A.M., no matter what time it is, is it just the clock that's broken, or the whole VCR?

Untimely from Utah

Dear Untimely:

What do you think this is, "Ask Mr. Wizard?" This is a handyman's guide, not a TV repair course. But since you asked, all you have to do is take a piece of duct tape and cover the flashing clock. Now insert a tape of "Viva Las Vegas" starring Elvis and punch the play button. If it plays, there's nothing wrong with your VCR; but you needn't worry about that. Unless you're smarter than most of us, you don't know how to set the timer on your VCR to tape a program anyway. The duct tape will keep you from being distracted by the flashing lights.

Dear Bubba:

Why are the directions for everything printed in a foreign language, even if you bought it at Home Depot?

Bewildered in Beaufort

Dear Bewildered:

I have asked several manufacturers about this, and their only explanation is a simple one. They have to buy the paper for the instructions in one size, which is usually too big. When they printed the directions in English only, they had all this white space, which looked funny, so one of the technical writers came up with the idea of printing the instructions in German, Spanish, French, and Serbo-Croatian. None of these products is sold in any of those countries, of course. If they were, the buyers would immediately recognize the fact that the directions don't mean anything at all. In fact, all of the directions are written by a committee in Japan (where all of the products are manufactured before being shipped here) who are still using a 1943 *Trick Webster's Dictionary* that was dropped on Tokyo by an American propaganda plane. The words are all backwards. Left means right and down means up. Counter-clockwise means clockwise. That's why you see such expressions as "Insert Tripod A into Hexagonal B and Tighten Nuts Severely."

Dear Bubba:

How come it is that batteries are *never* included? Is this some kind of Eveready plot?

Run Down in Roanoke

Dear Run Down:

In a word, yes, it's a plot. Haven't you noticed the Energizer bunny *everywhere?* You don't think he's going to be happy just interrupting commercials, do you? And furthermore, why *should* they include batteries? Your Mr. Coffee doesn't come with coffee, your Fry Daddy doesn't come with a father figure, and your lady Clairol doesn't come with Clairol. Get a life.

Dear Bubba:

Is there a natural law that men and women who are married to each other can't wallpaper a room without going after one another with blunt instruments?

No. 278143

Dear No. 278143:

No, there's no law that I know of, unless it was passed by the Georgia legislature last session. I have found that most of these domestic altercations are not a cause of the home improvement project in progress, but the result of a long-simmering grudge about the choice of honeymoon motels, the choice of snacks on a long family vacation, or failure to lower the toilet seat for twenty-four years. So the next time you want to blame an act of violence on wall-papering or painting, just remember: this is only a symptom. By the way, you may be surprised to know that I am familiar with your case, and, yes, I understand why you were so upset about your husband's wallpapering technique. Anybody who thinks it's unimportant if the two halves of the hippos don't match doesn't deserve to live.

———

Dear Bubba:

What's the difference between epoxy and grout? Can you get in bad trouble if you don't know?

Confused in Cobb

Dear Confused:

Obviously you have never watched "This Old House" or read Dr. Seuss. Epoxy is a very potent glue that is used to stick down everything from tile to dentures. A grout is an imaginary creature that once tried to steal Christmas. He would have been successful, too, if the elves had not spread epoxy all around Santa's workshop. So, yes, you could get in trouble if you don't know. Could you imagine what would happen if you tried to use a grout between your bathroom tiles instead of epoxy?

———

Dear Bubba:

If you buy paint at the paint store and then don't paint the room for a long time—say five or six years—will the paint store shake it up again on one of their machines for free? Will they laugh while they're doing it?

Unshaken in Union City

Dear Unshaken:

What are you, some kind of procrastinator? I'll bet you've got a closet full of wallpaper rolls that you meant to hang right after the honeymoon fourteen years ago. Well, tell me this. Are there rust spots on the cans? Has all of the printing on the labels faded? What's the expiration date? You obviously don't know this, but paint only has a shelf life of 3½ weeks. That's right. Those cans of eggnog, on the other hand, will keep for years. And yes, the men at the paint store will laugh if you bring in cans of six-year-old paint. But they will shake up your eggnog for free.

Dear Bubba:

What is a "spline tool," and does the average woman living alone need one?

Lonely in Lubbock

Dear Lonely:

I'm afraid that's something you'll have to decide for yourself, like whether to buy a handgun or a German shepherd. All I can tell you is that many of the widows and divorcées I have known eventually have had to buy a "spline tool" if they did not remarry within eighteen months. The only women who didn't buy "spline tools" moved in with unemployed roofers. Of course, everybody knows you can't replace a screen without one. A word of caution: "Spline tool" is not to be confused with "splain tool," which was a favorite expression of Ricky Ricardo on "I Love Lucy," or "Spine Tool," which is a delicate instrument used by graduates of Life Chiropractic College. By the way, thank you for including your address. The next time your spline needs adjusting, just give me a call.

Dear Bubba:

Why is it that Super Glue sticks to everything but what it's supposed to? How long does it take to let go, if you let it alone? Answer fast, please.
Stuck in Savannah

Dear Stuck:

Apparently you did not follow those microscopic directions on the tube, which clearly state in English, German, French, and Serbo-Croatian that the product sold is to be used only as directed. Did the directions say to put it on your fingertips and squeeze them together? Did the directions say to apply a thin bead on your mother-in-law's dentures and stick them to the nightstand? Did the directions say to put a drop on your sleeping husband's nose and then tickle it with a feather? No-oooo. So, Miss Stuck, I guess you are unless you are willing to send $347.50 to Bubba, in care of Earl's Eatery, Plum Branch, SC 29835. Cash orders for the Super Dooper Glue Remover will be processed the same day. Checks will take up to six weeks for delivery.

Dear Bubba:

Why isn't there a law against putting "Some Simple Assembly Required" on things sold in pieces?

Disassembled in Dayton

Dear Disassembled:

You're right. There should be, but because the Assemblers Union has such a powerful lobby, passage of such legislation is highly unlikely. I understand, however, that a referendum pending in Georgia would require every state candidate to assemble a gas grill using just a pair of pliers and a screwdriver before they will be allowed to run for office. The people who qualify probably won't be any smarter, but at least we'll know they're manually dexterous. Or was he the guy who ran the dessert shop on Fourteenth Street?

Dear Bubba:

Would it be a bad thing if you're doing a little simple electrical work, and you don't know where the circuit breaker is, so you don't turn 'em off because you don't want to ask somebody?

Befuddled in Brunswick

Dear Befuddled:

No, there is no need to turn off the circuit breakers if you have a valid will and have decided that your wife is never going to lose weight and your grown children are never going to get jobs and leave home. In that case, I suggest you wear steel-toed boots and dampen them thoroughly, since this will provide an excellent conductor for the electricity. Otherwise, if you want to live to change another fuse, I suggest you locate the circuit breaker box, flip every switch, pull on rubber-soled shoes, and dial the number for the nearest qualified electrician.

Dear Bubba:

Are television antennas grounded? Can you work on them in the rain, as long as it's not raining too hard?
                              Fuzzy in Fairbanks

Dear Fuzzy:

You're a "Geraldo" fan, aren't you? Okay, in that case, the best time to work on a TV antenna is during a violent thunderstorm. That's what Ben Franklin did, and look what happened to him. He went bald and was appointed ambassador to France. Wouldn't you like to go to France? Wouldn't you like to be a member of the Hair Club? Wouldn't you like to become a cable TV subscriber so you won't have to make a fool of yourself by asking these stupid questions and can spend your time instead watching the Home Shopping Network or the juicer infomercials?

Dear Bubba:

If you buy a kit that says, "So Simple Even a Child Can Do It," and you can't, does this say bad things about you?
Uncoordinated in Utica

Dear Uncoordinated:

Not necessarily. Some of the products with that label are so complicated Thomas Edison would have given up before he understood how they worked. You have to understand that the people who make up these labels are the same ones who were teachers' pets in fifth grade and who always set up the audiovisual equipment. They later wore those plastic pocket protectors with fourteen ballpoint pens and wore dark horn-rimmed glasses. They are making lots more money than we are, but they have no sex lives and have never seen an Ingmar Bergman movie that they understood. There. Does that make you feel better about not being able to figure out how to use the Amazing Veg-o-Matic?

Dear Bubba:

I know you're not a lawyer, but is it grounds for divorce if the color on the Sherwin-Williams paint chip looks different on the wall?
Seeing Red in Seattle

Dear Seeing:

Not unless your husband was the Sherwin-Williams salesman who sold you the paint. By the way, I think you should lighten up here. What is this room, anyway? The bedroom? Isn't it always dark in there? The living room? Who uses the living room anymore except when you have to invite in encyclopedia salesmen and Jehovah's Witnesses, and what do they know about color? The bathroom? Are you kidding? Unless it's a hideous shade of fuchsia, who's going to notice? Oh. It is a hideous shade of fuchsia? In that case, unless you have caught your husband in a body-painting episode with a hooker at the Half-Day Inn, forget the divorce and put up some wallpaper.

Dear Bubba:

If you've already painted your whole house, didn't prime it, didn't sand it, and didn't treat it for mildew first, what should you do?

Distressed in Dallas

Dear Distressed:

Sounds like you done messed up big. Can you sell your house before rainy season? Before Saturday? Very well. Stucco is a good alternative, or you could simply repaint with one of the new exterior paint shades: Mildew Madness. Add some Green Mold shutters and you'll probably be featured in the home and garden section of your local newspaper.

Dear Bubba:

If electrical plugs are either female or male, why isn't the world buried in little pluglets?

Electrified in Elberton

Dear Electrified:

This is a trick question, isn't it? I asked some of my electrician friends, and they say that most of these plugs are insulated with rubber coatings and a ground prong. (No, I'm not going to touch that one with a ten-amp pole.) It's not as exciting as an unprotected coupling, but it prevents a lot of short circuits and, as you so delicately put it, a population explosion of little pluglets.

Dear Bubba:

If the tag on the stepladder says, "Do Not Stand on the Top Step," what is the top step for? Can you sue if you did it anyway?

Laid Up in Louisiana

Dear Laid:

Yes, ordinarily the top step is not to be used, but it's there for a purpose, just like the warning flashers on your car. In case of an emergency, such as when you have to reach way up high to paint a spot on your ceiling or your child's helium balloon is caught in the chandelier or your girlfriend's cat is stranded in the top of a plum tree. Even then, you should proceed with caution and get the skinny kid from next door to stand on the top step while you hold the ladder securely. Or you could get your brother-in-law to stand on it while you hold it for a minute then wander off to get a Coke. No, you can't sue. Not unless you're a stepchild or a stepparent.

———

Dear Bubba:

The TV ads say those hardware men are both helpful and friendly, but is it normal for them to offer to come to my house to fix things for free after 10:00 P.M.?

Busty Widow in Buffalo

Dear Busty:

You must be referring to Harvey, the Happy Helpful Horny Hardware man. Harvey's motto is simple: "If you're a good-looking woman with a problem, then Baby, I'm your handyman." Not every hardware store has a Harvey, so I guess you're just lucky. My suggestion is to let Harvey come over after ten only if you have a big burly brother who can stand over him while he cleans out your drain, repairs your furnace, and takes care of all those pesky little jobs that have been bothering you for years.

Chapter 17

HOW TO TURN YOUR FAMILY ROOM INTO A TAVERN

(And Other Weekend Projects So Simple Even Your Brother-in-Law Can Do Them)

THERE'S A FAMOUS country music song in which the female singer, obviously frustrated by her husband's nocturnal habits, threatens to hire a wino to decorate their home. Don't laugh. This is really not such a bad idea. In big cities and small towns all across the country, people who have more money than taste are converting perfectly good dens and basements into tacky game rooms with cheap paneling and swag lamps and Ping-Pong tables.

Well, you, too, can join this fashionable trend and provide a comfortable place for your friends to gather. No longer will your wife wonder where you are and whether you are sober enough to drive home. You'll be a few feet away from the kitchen, slumped over a card table with three of your unemployed neighbors.

Right now you are probably saying, "Bubba, this is a good idea for somebody with a bagful of money and a working wife, but you're talking about some big bucks here."

Not necessarily.

In fact, you may already have most of the things you need. After all, you're not creating a British gentleman's club. You're making an approximate likeness of a sleazy beer joint. If all goes well, you'll be the talk of the neighborhood. Your local paper will probably want to take pictures and do a spread in the home and garden section under the headline "Honky Tonk Chic."

Best of all, this project requires no wall demolition and little sawing and hammering. It does require a little ingenuity and imagination.

WHAT YOU'LL NEED

- A 30-inch wide interior hollow-core door. If you can find a solid wood door that's not too expensive and has an undecorated surface, go ahead and buy that. It'll last longer.
- Six or eight cases of beer.
- Animal heads, preferably ones that have been prepared by a taxidermist
- A couple of lighted beer signs, especially ones that have little bubbles floating around in them. Check with your local beer distributor about buying these, go to flea markets, or visit a nearby college campus. Usually male students have them in their dorm rooms.

- A couple of pub tables that you can pick up at a flea market
- Four or five barstools, used
- Rickety wooden chairs (four to eight)
- Ashtrays
- A jukebox (Okay, I know these are expensive, but not nearly as expensive as tearing out a wall and adding a solarium.)
- Tacky post cards with risqué messages
- A selection of country music songs (tear-jerkers and Western swing)
- Cut-out pictures of country music stars
- Glossy-coat polyurethane
- A framed velvet picture of Elvis
- Several 15- or 25-watt light bulbs for that dimly lit look
- Cheap parquet flooring or linoleum

WHAT TO DO

The first thing you should do is get rid of all your good furniture. Move it into other parts of the house or give it to Goodwill. Take down all pictures of your family and put up ones of Elvis, Hank Williams, Jr., and Dolly Parton, along with an assortment of animal heads.

If you have carpet, rip it out and replace it with cheap parquet wood flooring or linoleum.

Replace all the light bulbs with ones that have lower wattage.

Build your bar by stacking cases of beer in two stacks, about six feet apart, until they are the appropriate height. Take the door you have brought, sand it well, glue the cut-out pictures of country music stars and cheap postcards on the top, and then decoupage by coating the door with

the glossy polyurethane. Let dry, then place your bar across the stacks of beer cases.

Clear out the books on your bookcase directly behind the bar and replace them with a few bottles of whiskey and mixers.

Set up your pub tables and cheap, wobbly chairs in an attractive arrangement, line up the barstools at the bar, plug in the jukebox, set a dish of roasted peanuts on the bar, drag in a cooler of ice for the long-neck beer, and make your wife dress up like a barmaid. Now you're ready to invite the neighbors over with the satisfaction that what you have done is not only unique, it performs a valuable community service by keeping the drunks off the streets and in your back yard.

Now if you can just talk your wife out of decorating your bedroom in the style of a nineteenth-century San Francisco brothel. . . .

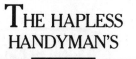

WEEKEND PROJECTS

A Double-Wide Purple Martin Home

There is nothing more irritating than watching a family of purple martins or chickadees living like rich Republicans or American automobile executives while you and your loved ones have to make do in something from Honest Ed's Pre-fabricated Residences on Wheels. Honest Ed's motto is: "Why pay rent when you can own your own home for $47 down and $47 a week?" What Honest Ed doesn't tell you is that you will be paying long after his cheap paneling has turned to sawdust.

Yes, I know you bought it as a temporary shelter while you were saving up the down payment for your two-story Williamsburg mansion in Tara Estates. But that was seventeen years ago, and the little woman is getting a mite irritable with the present accommodations, which would cramp a family of sardines. Especially when she has to navigate between your new Bassmaster sixteen-foot boat and your slightly used 1991 Ford Bronco with the monster wheels, and then has to step over the rotten board in the

front porch, the one that Aunt Mabel stuck her size twelve foot through, to get inside the trailer.

Well, here's a way to take her mind off the thin walls, the sagging floors, and the drooling rug rats. Make an exact birdhouse replica of your mobile home. After all, if it's good enough for you and the family, it's good enough for a flock of nomadic martins. Besides, having your own double-wide mobile home birdhouse will be a real conversation piece when your drinking buddies come over to shoot at rats off the back deck.

Build several of them, and you can have your own trailer park. But be careful. If you skimp on the materials and details, you'll run the risk of making the same mistake as Lamar. His double-wide martin houses were so shoddy that he attracted some of the laziest birds you ever saw, the ruby-necked white thrashers. Lamar said all they did was hang around the nests and wait for a bug to drop dead. Then, after a considerable amount of discussion, one of the ruby-necked white thrashers wandered over and picked it up. Before long, the whole lot of them was chased out by a bunch of migrant sparrows.

WHAT YOU'LL NEED

- 1 x 12 (16 feet) board
- 1½-inch pipe flange
- 1½-inch galvanized pipe
- 4-penny galvanized finishing nails (about a handful)
- Waterproof glue
- Gray paint (or a color to match your mobile home)
- A set of wheels from Lamar, Jr.'s old Tonka truck
- One trailer tongue from an old toy (or make your own with a flat piece of lathe or scrap wood)
- ⅝-inch dowel (eighteen inches long)

HOW TO MAKE IT

Saw a 20-inch piece of the 1 x 12 board for the bottom. Watch your fingers, and make sure you measured it right. That's twenty inches, Lamar.

Now cut two 22-inch pieces from the 1 x 12. Set up your neighbor's table saw to rip one of the boards to ten inches wide and the other to 9½ inches. These are going to be your roof.

Cut the ends by sawing off a two-foot section from the rest of the 1 x 12 and rip down to 9½ inches. Now cut this piece into two 11⅝-inch pieces. These will be your end pieces, and they need to be cut at 45-degree angles for the roof. The easy way to do that is to mark the center point at the top of each of the end pieces (4⅝ inches). Draw a straight line from the center mark at the top to 7¾-inch marks on the edge. For the front and back, cut two more pieces 18½ inches long. (That's because you subtract the thickness of the end pieces. You'll see what I mean when you start to put it together.) Set your table saw to cut the tops of the boards at a 45-degree angle so you can nail your roof on (See diagram).

To set up perches, measure 2½ inches from the bottom and 4 inches from each side. Drill ⅝-inch holes for the dowel perches, then 1½ inches above these holes drill 1-inch entry holes.

Now you're ready to cut the inside partition. That's right—even purple martins need their privacy. Cut a 15½-inch partition from the remaining 1 x 12 board.

If all has gone well, you should have all your pieces ready to assemble. This is a good time to yell into the house for your wife to stop cooking the squash soufflé and come outside and help you hold the boards. Or else stomp inside, shaking sawdust over the freshly swept linoleum, and pry the headphones off your teenage son's ears while he listens to the latest from Def Leppard and the Dead Cat Trio or whatever his favorite group is.

Nail the pieces together with the 4-penny nails, starting with the base, then the sides and ends. Now put the partition in the middle of the house and nail in place. Add a little glue to all the joints to make sure they don't pull apart. Now cut four pieces of the dowel about 2½ inches long and glue in place. *Make sure they are flush with the inside of the house.*

Borrow some caulking from your neighbor for the roof joint, add the wheels and the trailer tongue, and paint the same color as your trailer. If this doesn't impress your wife as much as that stuffed raccoon you gave her last Christmas, I don't know what will.

Virgil Underwood's Under-the-Bed Storage Unit

There was a time when I was growing up that beds were at least eighteen inches off the floor with plenty of room underneath to play hide-and-seek. Since my mother and my two aunts swept, dusted, and mopped every forty-eight minutes, there weren't even any dust bunnies to get caught in your hair. My mother never would have considered actually storing clothes and things under the bed. That's what barns were for.

Whenever I couldn't find some of my clothes or my valuable keepsakes like an autographed picture of the Lone Ranger and Sky King's Turquoise Thunderbird Mine Ring, I'd ask Mama where they were.

"They're in the barn," she'd say.

"What part?"

"Back in there behind the meat box."

Now, if you've never been inside an honest-to-goodness country barn, you will find this experience beyond belief. The closest thing to exploring a barn just before nightfall is sitting through a Stephen King double feature.

Our barn had two large storage rooms, a big hayloft, a wagon shed, and four animal stalls. The important stuff, like harnesses and sweet feed and corn, went into the first room. The second room was my uncle's junk room. We had two hog-butchering tables stacked in there, a meat box where we buried hams in salt to let them cure, hog wire, barbed wire, two old radios, three chain saws in various stages of disassembly, two trunkfuls of carnival prizes and war memorabilia, a box of *Stag* magazines (well used), assorted nails, screws, farm implements, barn cats, stray puppies, and spiders the size of a watermelon. Well, maybe I exaggerate, but not by much.

Also somewhere in there were my old toys that my mama got tired of picking up in the yard. I would enter the barn with my heart in my throat and a large hunting knife in my right hand. If Tarzan could subdue sixteen-foot crocodiles with his knife, I saw no reason that I could not handle a couple of stubborn spiders with mine.

I swung the door open as far as I could and saw immediately that I should have brought a flashlight. Why are barns always so dark? Anyway, I picked my way through my uncle's junk and spotted the box that contained my prized possessions. I carefully opened the top, fished out my Sky King Lost Thunderbird Silver Mine Turquoise Ring and my autographed picture of the Lone Ranger (Tonto was always referring to the masked man as Kemo Sabe. It took me years to find out, but it actually is a Native American term of endearment that, loosely translated, means "white man who sleeps in women's undergarments"), and I was about to beat a hasty retreat when I saw a dog-eared copy of Errol Flynn's autobiography, *My Wicked Wicked Ways.* I thought Mama had burned it along with my paperback copy of *Peyton Place* with the carefully marked passages, but she had simply hidden it. I sat down on my uncle's old Army trunk and began to read about Errol's exploits. Suddenly it got real dark, and I heard the latch on the door being fastened. I shouted and lunged for the door at the same time, tripping over a part of a chain saw and falling on a half-blind tomcat.

My father repaired the broken door and buried the cat without asking me for any details. The cat was about

twenty-three years old and had begun to think he was a mouse, so it really was a mercy killing. But looking back on that experience, I realize now that all of that could have been avoided if my mother had just allowed us to store our junk under the bed.

If you are living in a house without adequate storage (and according to every woman I talk to, there is *never* enough storage), you might consider constructing an under-the-bed drawer like the one Virgil Underwood built. Virgil's a bachelor, see, and he likes everything to be real neat. When the first cool weather hits, he gathers up all of his summer clothes except one outfit and packs them away in one of his under-the-bed units. Then when spring comes, he puts away all of his winter clothes. Virgil lined his under-the-bed drawer with strips of cedar to keep away the moths.

WHAT YOU'LL NEED

First, measure your bed to see what dimensions to make your drawer. Then buy 1 sheet of ¾-inch plywood sanded on one side. Actually, if you can get them to saw it thirty inches wide by whatever length you need it, that will be a lot easier. They'll do this at most building warehouses for 25 cents a cut.

Get two pieces of 1 x 6 board cut to the length of the plywood plus four inches; two 1 x 4 side pieces no longer than thirty-inches each; 2 pieces of 2 x 2 cut to the length of the 1 x 4 pieces; four two-inch casters and two pull handles (These can be wooden knobs or hardware that fits on most drawers; or you can get it to match the hardware on your other bedroom furniture).

HOW TO MAKE IT

Assemble with two-inch drywall screws and wood glue by attaching the 2 x 2 cleats to the tops of the side pieces. Before putting the entire unit together, measure to make sure the bottom will have at least one-half-inch clearance off the floor once the casters are attached to the cleats. Now join sides to the bottom with the screws and add the front and back. Put your casters on, drill holes for the handles, and sand and stain before you attach the handles.

If you want to store woolen clothes, either prepare to

use mothballs or pick up some cedar strips at the building supply place and tack them on the inside of the drawer. Sand the strips periodically to keep the smell strong. I don't know why moths don't like cedar; it smells wonderful to me.

Screw on the handles, and now you're ready to fill it up with clothes that are too small, bell-bottom jeans, a Nehru jacket that you hope will come back into style, and the pictures from the honeymoon that you should have burned but you didn't. But if you ever decide to find a better hiding place from your nosy kids, let me know. I've got a barn with spiders the size of watermelons.

Charles "Deuce" Carter's Card Table

There is nothing like a friendly game of poker to break up the boredom of watching "America's Funniest Home Videos" or reruns of "Mr. Ed" on those long weekends when the only sporting events on TV are games in which grown men skate around in circles and try to knock each other's teeth out with long sticks. Occasionally, someone will take out his frustration on something called a puck, which looks like one of Uncle Jethro's second wife's biscuits.

Unfortunately, when I was growing up, my mother (very sensibly, I realize now) banned any card games in which money changed hands. "That's gambling," she said one day when I was ahead of my Uncle Jim by $6.25. She proceeded to rake all the money off the table into her apron. Then she burned the cards.

From then on, we were restricted to playing Scrabble, checkers, or *Monotony*, which is a white trash variation of Monopoly. You rent out tenant shacks, buy used mobile homes, and increase your income by selling moonshine and hunting dogs or by leasing your unmarried daughters to visiting businessmen. This is a game in which the players try to get sent to jail.

Anyway, the one thing I regretted was that we didn't have a real card table. We could play on the kitchen table after the dinner dishes were cleared, but the women were still in there and we men couldn't tell dirty jokes. Or we could go out on the porch and lay a square piece of plywood on a stool and use that.

It wasn't until I was well into high school that I played cards on a real card table. This was at Charles ("Deuce") Carter's house. Deuce was one of my boyhood idols. He drove a Corvette, used English Leather, and knew how to make mixed drinks. I had my first whiskey sour at Deuce's house, heard my first Dave Brubeck record, and saw my first *Playboy* centerfold.

I'm grateful to Deuce for all these things, but most of all, I'm grateful to him for what he taught me about gambling.

Don't do it.

Or if you do, make sure you know your limits. And never, *never* play with a man who wears an eye patch and can shuffle the deck with one hand. Deuce could shuffle with one hand, and he had an eye patch. For years I thought he had gotten his eye put out in the war, although I was never clear what war Deuce had fought in. Then I heard he had dueled a fencing champion from Yale over a woman and lost his eye. I was certainly disappointed to learn later that he had shot himself in the eye with a Red Ryder BB gun when he was nine.

Despite this handicap, Deuce lived a good life. He owned his own home, went to all the Carolina football games, dated an Alabama majorette, and water-skied every summer. Plus, he had one of the nicest card tables I ever saw.

"Made it myself," he said proudly one day when I was admiring it. He rubbed his hand across the top. "Real vinyl," he laughed. "None of that tacky calf hide."

He's gone now, a victim of a poor loser in a high-stakes game in Augusta, but I managed to salvage the plans for his card table. I just hope that if you build it, you have better luck than Deuce.

WHAT YOU'LL NEED

- A piece of ¾-inch plywood 36 x 36 inches
- A piece of vinyl upholstery at least 40 inches square
- Four pieces of 1 x 3 x 40-inch wood trim (pine or whatever kind you like and can afford)
- Four ready-made legs and screw-on attachments

HOW TO MAKE IT

To glue the vinyl on the plywood, first thin some white glue with a little water and use a paintbrush to spread it evenly over the plywood. Lay the vinyl upside down on a

flat surface. Now lay the plywood on the vinyl, glue side down, and center it.

Pull one end of the vinyl over the edge of the board, stretch and staple with a staple gun. Put in as many staples as you think it needs. Do this around the other sides, too. On the corners, fold the vinyl, tuck, cut off the excess with scissors or a razor knife, and staple. Using C-clamps, clamp the vinyl-covered board to another flat surface and let it dry overnight.

Measure the 1 x 3 trim to fit around the edge of the table and miter cut at 45 degrees. Attach with paneling nails and glue. Countersink the nails and fill in with plastic wood that can be sanded and finished later.

Now screw on the four plates that hold the ready-made legs you bought, attach the legs, sand, seal, or stain to match the trim, and you're ready to deal. But for goodness sake, don't try to draw to an inside straight, don't play cards with women (unless it's strip poker), and never try to bluff a man with an eye patch who drinks whiskey sours and shuffles with one hand.

Fred Firestone's Firewood Rack

For years, Fred Firestone supplemented his income from working at the poultry processing plant by cutting firewood for folks. Unfortunately, Fred was so busy cutting wood for everybody else that he always ran short himself. That bothered his wife Edna a lot since Edna is naturally a high-strung woman who flies into a rage when somebody gets in the express lane with thirteen grocery items or when little old ladies with walkers get stuck in the middle of the street when the traffic light changes. You've seen those cowcatchers on the front of locomotives? Well, Edna has a senior citizen disperser on the front of her Buick Electra.

Anyway, the last thing Fred wanted to do, other than slicing off his middle finger with the chain saw, was to get Edna's dander up. So he did what any other spineless husband would have done. After he finished cutting firewood for everybody, he went over to Johnson's Lumber Yard in Augusta and bought a load of seasoned split red oak. What's wrong with that, you say? Have you ever smelled split red oak? There's no way to describe it, but if you have a cat, take a whiff of his potty box. There's little difference between the smells.

Now Fred knew Edna would never let him put any of that oak in the porch, and he didn't want it to lie out in the elements and get damp every time it rained; so he was forced to build a covered firewood rack. It's a little more sophisticated than the one I use, which is two poles laid down on the ground between four other poles. I stack the wood on the two poles and throw a tarp over it when I finish. It's not pretty, but it does the job.

If you're a suburbanite, though, and you want your yard to look respectable, go ahead and follow Fred's plan.

WHAT YOU'LL NEED

- One sheet of ¾-inch exterior grade plywood 4 x 8 feet
- Six treated 10-foot-long 2 x 4 boards
- Seven eight-foot-long treated 2 x 4 boards
- A couple of pounds of galvanized 16-penny nails
- One large box of ¾-inch roofing nails
- Thirty-two 1¼-inch flathead wood screws
- Eight 2½-inch flathead wood screws
- One roll of roofing paper
- Two bundles of roofing shingles

HOW TO MAKE IT

Use the 2 x 4 boards to make the bottom frame. Cut eight 4¾-inch spacers and two 20¼-inch end pieces. Nail the spacers to the middle rails first (so it will be easy to nail; you'll see), then nail the middle rails to the middle spacers. Now nail the outside rails and attach the end rails.

Lay the bottom frame on the spot where you want the woodshed to be located and drive a stake at each inside corner of the frame. Now move the frame, dig four holes about 20- to 24-inches deep, throw in a small flat rock or some gravel, and move the frame back in place. Now insert the four posts through the frame into the holes. Slide some bricks under the frame to make it level. Cut the four posts to their proper lengths and reinsert them in the holes. Make sure they're plumb, and then attach them to

the frame with four carriage bolts. Now add dirt to the holes and tamp firmly.

Fasten two 8-foot-long 2 x 4 boards at the top of the posts (flush) with 16-penny nails.

To make your roof trusses, take the plywood and cut four pieces. Two will be triangular, 34¼ inches long by 9⅞ inches high. Mark a point in the center and cut at 45 degrees on each side.

You'll need to cut the inside trusses smaller, since they're going on the inside of the frame. Cut two pieces from the plywood 20¼ inches wide by 9⅞ inches high. Cut a 1½ x 3½-inch notch from the bottom on each side. Now measure the midpoint at the top and make a 30-degree miter cut on each side.

Attach the end trusses with 1¼-inch screws and the middle trusses with 2½-inch screws. The tops of the trusses should align.

Cut two strips of the plywood 8 feet long and wide enough to cover each side of the roof.

The strips should overlap by 2⅜ inches on each end and should be fastened with the 1¼-inch screws.

Add the roofing felt, nail down with the roofing nails, and cover with shingles according to the instructions on the shingle bundle.

Bubba's Bird Feeder

The next time an anniversary or your wife's birthday rolls around, don't rush out to the nearest jewelry store and spend twenty or thirty dollars on some expensive trinket. Give her something that will be useful, decorative, and politically correct—a bird feeder.

I know, you're probably saying right now that you hope this bird feeder is not too large because you have an idea where your wife is going to suggest you put it. But don't be too hasty. Remember, it's the thought that counts. And in this case, explain that you are giving her a gift that will attract feathered creatures that are almost as beautiful as

she is. Every time you look out the window and see a cardinal or a blue jay pecking at the feed, you'll think of her. Then give her a big hug. If that doesn't work, write me, and I'll send you a copy of my next book, *How to Jump-Start Your Romance Without Using a Cattle Prod.*

WHAT YOU'LL NEED

- A 4½-inch or 5-inch diameter hardwood log
- One screw-in eyehook sturdy enough to support the hanging log
- One dowel rod ¼ inch in diameter and 9 or 10 inches long
- Heavy twine or galvanized wire, as much as needed to reach a good-sized limb to hang the feeder on

HOW TO MAKE IT

This really is simple. Go out to your neighbor's woodpile (preferably when no one's home) and select a nice log that has slick bark. Not pine.

Using an ax or hatchet, taper the ends and then bore two or three 1¾-inch diameter holes about 1½ inches deep. Now, 1½ inches below the big holes, drill ¼-inch holes about ¾ inch deep. These are for your dowel pegs, which you will cut about 3 inches long and insert in small holes for the birds to perch on.

Now saw off enough of one of the tapered ends to make a flat place to screw in the eyehook. Make a little hole to start the screw by driving an 8-penny common nail in a little way and pulling it out.

Get some suet from your butcher and stuff the holes. Now attach your heavy twine or wire to the eyehook, and hang the feeder off the end of your porch or a nearby limb.

Paulette Peablossom's Plant Caddy

Paulette Peablossom has won the Greater Plum Branch Garden Club "Best Yard" award six times in a row. Her jealous neighbor, Lurleen Hash, says it's because Paulette spends more time in her flower bed than in her marriage bed. That may be so, but you won't hear Peterson Peablossom complaining. Peterson hurt his back several years ago trying to bring in Paulette's potted palm when there was a frost warning one night, so that relieved him of some of his marital duties. But Paulette wasn't about to

give up her gardening. She made Peterson build her several plant caddies so he could roll them in and out of the house without straining his back.

Rest assured that these are not fancy pieces of furniture. Peterson is not what you would call a skilled craftsman or a brilliant thinker. He flunked high school shop because he couldn't build a shoeshine kit, and he was one of the few members of the Future Farmers of America who never mastered the art of swine judging. But once again Peterson Peablossom proves that even a hapless handyman can construct a functional piece of furniture. The only problem is, every time Peterson builds one of these, Paulette goes out and buys another plant that is only slightly smaller than Rhode Island.

WHAT YOU'LL NEED

- Four pieces of 2 x 14½-inch pine lattice (that thin ¼-inch stuff)
- Four pieces of 2 x 14¼-inch pine lattice
- Four pieces of 1½ x 1½ x 11¾-inch pine boards
- Eight pieces of ¾ x 1½ x 10½-inch pine boards
- Four pieces of ¼ x 13¾ x 14-inch plywood
- One piece of ¾ x 13½ x 13½-inch plywood
- Four rollers or casters for the bottom

HOW TO MAKE IT

Use 1¼-inch drywall screws (rub the ends on soap to make them screw in easier) to attach the bottom and side braces to each of the four sides. (Install the rails flush with the tops of the sides; the bottom rails will be 2¼ inches from the bottom edge of the sides. This is so the casters will be hidden. You'll see.)

Now get someone to help you hold each side against the bottom and use 1½-inch drywall screws to attach the corners of the bottom panel to the braces. Once this is done and you have a nice box, all you have to do is measure the outside edges of the caddy and cut the top pine lattice trim at 45-degree angles. (If your neighbor doesn't have a good miter saw or miter box, you need to buy one of the cheap ones along with a stiff-back miter saw.) The best way to do this is to cut the first two pieces to fit on opposite sides (lay flat on top of the caddy flush with the inside edge), nail with 3-penny finishing nails (add a little glue if you have it), then measure the distance between and cut the remaining two pieces.

Now cut the trim that goes underneath this trim (you don't really have to do this, but it makes it look a little better) and nail in place with 3-penny finish nails. Sand, paint, or stain with a couple of coats, and add the casters on the bottom. All that's left is to add a suitably large plant and wait for it to shed its leaves all over your carpet.

A Lazy Bubba

I know these items are usually called lazy Susans, but I figured there was no reason they couldn't be modified to take care of a hungry man's needs. Roy Bill's wife Eleanor bought a lazy Susan recently, and set it on their nice round oak table.

"What are you going to put on that?" Roy Bill asked.

"Condiments," Eleanor said.

"Say what?"

"Condiments," Eleanor said, glancing at her husband's shocked expression. "Oh, for goodness' sakes, Bubba, explain to Roy Bill what a condiment is while I put up the groceries."

"Is it what I think it is?" Roy Bill said once Eleanor left the room.

"Sort of," I said. "A condiment is candy that is served after you make love using protection."

"Eleanor's going to put those on the dining room table?"

"That's what she said."

A few minutes later, Eleanor brought out catsup, oil and vinegar, salt and pepper, mustard, and a jumbo bottle of Texas Pete hot sauce (Roy Bill likes his food spicy) and put them on the lazy Susan.

"Where are you going to put the condom mints?" Roy Bill asked.

"These are the condiments," Eleanor said, exasperated. "I swear, you're the only two grown men I've ever met whose IQs are less than room temperature."

Roy Bill grinned and wiped his brow with his handkerchief. "Is it hot in here to you, Bubba?"

"Feels like it to me. It must be at least 140 degrees."

WHAT YOU'LL NEED

The easiest way to make this is to go to a building supply warehouse like Home Depot and buy one 18-inch and one 12-inch wood circle already cut and shaped. These are the 5/4-inch thick ones. Check your local hardware store for a swivel bearing mount (or you can order them from mail order houses, any woodworking supply magazine or catalog).

You'll also need six or eight small Shaker pegs to put around the edge of the lazy Bubba to keep things from sliding off, like your jar of Penrose hot sausages, your pickled eggs, or your dish of roasted peanuts.

HOW TO MAKE IT

First, drill holes around the edge of the large circle to accommodate your Shaker pegs (measure the bottoms of the pegs and find a drill bit to match). Sand the circles and stain them (it's easier to do it now than after you put everything together). When they are dry, glue in the Shaker pegs and stain them. Attach the swivel bearing mount according to directions on the package. Or, if you can't find a swivel mount, you can drill a ¾-inch hole about halfway into the bottom of the top part and a ⅞-inch hole halfway in the top of the bottom part. Cut a piece of ¾-inch dowel about 1¾-inches long. Glue one end in the ¾-inch hole on the top and insert in the bottom hole. Add a lttle candle wax to cut down on the friction, and it should perform adequately.

One word of warning: If you have friends over who are prone to drink a little too much, keep them away from the lazy Bubba. Ansel Crosshatch and Junior Stebbins came over to watch the Super Bowl and got so excited they spun the lazy Bubba too fast. I'm still finding pieces of pickled eggs and hot sausages under the furniture. But you know what? I believe the taste has improved with age.

Portulaca's Paper Towel Holder

Portulaca Peterson is one of those women who can't stand to see anything go to waste, especially her husband Roscoe. That poor man has more projects going than Bob Vila. Portulaca saves everything, from old newspapers to pieces of twine to those little twist ties off loaf bread bags. She saves broom handles, too, for closet rods, rug-beaters, and paper towel holders. Yes, even Roscoe has to admit Portulaca was environmentally correct before anyone ever heard of the greenhouse effect.

WHAT YOU'LL NEED

- One broomstick, preferably from a worn-out broom
- One piece of wood, about 6 inches square. You can use a 2 x 6-inch piece of pine, or glue together a couple of blocks of fancy wood like birch or maple or walnut. Portulaca prefers the pine since it's cheap.

HOW TO MAKE IT

Cut off the top section of the broom handle, about 12 inches long. Measure the diameter carefully, or hold a drill bit up to the end to check the size. Now mark a point square in the middle of the block of wood and drill a hole about 1 inch deep (assuming you have a 2-inch block of wood or two ¾-inch blocks glued together). Put some good wood glue in the hole and on the end of the broomstick (not the rounded end). Insert and let dry. Sand and paint a nice antique color like Wedgewood blue and you

have a perfectly good paper towel holder to set on your counter or carry with you out to the charcoal grill or to the fish-cleaning table—wherever it's needed.

Weldon Wall's Wall Shelf

Weldon Wall was one of the biggest collectors I knew when I was growing up in Plum Branch, South Carolina. He collected inkwells, antique radios, clocks, and those little glass insulators from old telephone poles. Weldon's wife Wynona would have preferred that Weldon keep his collectibles in the attic or barn loft, but Weldon liked to have his things out in the open so he could admire them in any room of the house. Of course, if you saw Wynona, you'd know why Weldon liked to look at old inkwells and glass insulators. Wynona was third runner-up in the Miss Cloverine Salve contest back in 1958, but they only had two contestants.

Wynona's hobbies are keeping a messy house, eating, and pointing out Weldon's flaws, which, as Wynona says, would be a full-time job by itself.

If you are a collector like Weldon or if your wife has a fondness for knickknacks, you might consider putting up a few wall shelves. At least everything is out in plain view, which is a real comfort when your sticky-fingered cousins are visiting.

WHAT YOU'LL NEED

If you really don't want to fool with a lot of cutting and measuring and you feel flush with last week's overtime check, drop by Home Depot or another fine building supply warehouse and buy a few pieces of precut, prerouted shelving with precut wooden brackets. All you have to do is screw them together, sand thoroughly with fine sand-

WONDER IF MY
ANTIQUE ANVIL
WOULD FIT UP THERE..?

paper, and add a couple of coats of polyurethane satin or glossy finish.

For the masochist, however, who wants to do everything from scratch, wander over to the lumber section and pick out a couple of 1 x 6-inch boards clear of too many knots. The length doesn't matter much. An 8-foot board is good for one 3-foot shelf.

HOW TO MAKE IT

Cut the board in 36-inch lengths and screw together in an L-shape using 1¼-inch drywall screws. Drill a small ¹⁄₁₆-inch pilot hole for the screws and the wood won't split. Also rake the screws across a bar of soap, and they'll screw in real easily.

For the brackets, use the leftover pieces from the 1 x 6 by cutting two pieces 5¼ inches long at a 45-degree angle. Position about 3 inches from each end and attach to the back of the shelf brace and top with 1¼-inch drywall screws. If you want it to look fancy, countersink the ones on top and fill in with plastic wood. Otherwise, nobody's going to be climbing up on a chair looking at the top of the shelf, so it doesn't matter if the screws show.

Now sand and stain the shelf or paint it in your favorite color to match the rest of the decor and fasten it to the wall about twelve to eighteen inches from the ceiling with 1½-inch drywall screws in a straight line. Then you can cover the screw heads by cutting a piece of decorative molding to fit and finishing to match the rest of the shelf.

If you really want to fancy it up, add three wooden Shaker pegs (check your building supply store or order them through a woodworking magazine) or fancy brass coat hooks.

Bubba's Boot Cleaner

How many times has your wife told you to wipe your muddy feet before coming in the back door? And how many times have you unsuccessfully tried to scrape off that stubborn red clay on those inadequate welcome mats? Well, here's one solution that worked for me and is a lot of fun to make.

WHAT YOU'LL NEED

- Two pieces of 1 x 3-foot exterior plywood.
- A couple of handfuls of ¾-inch or ½-inch roofing nails, or any nail with a big, flat head (no, Lamar, that wasn't meant as an insult to you).

- Go to your friendly neighborhood tavern after a Friday or Saturday night and ask to go through the trash to get a batch of those beer bottle caps. Or, you can do what Roy Bill did and just buy a couple of cases of long-necked beer and remove each cap individually.

HOW TO MAKE IT

Now screw together the two boards with 1-inch screws and attach the bottle caps, open side up, by nailing them onto the boards in any pattern that pleases you.

Place it outside the back door, and use it to scrape your boots or shoes. A few squirts from a garden hose cleans off the mud. You'll still need to wipe your feet on the welcome mat, but at least most of the muck will be removed by then.

Thelma Thornwell's Trivets

Thelma Thornwell is one of the best cooks in the Snellville area. She's a widow now, and all of her children have grown up and moved away. So Thelma is suffering from what psychologists today call the empty nest syndrome. Thelma just calls it being lonesome.

The worst thing about being alone, Thelma says, is not having anybody to cook for. One of the happiest days of her life was when a school bus carrying the Ware Shoals Wildcats football team took a wrong turn after the game and broke down in front of Thelma's farmhouse. While they were waiting for the wrecker and another bus, Thelma decided to whip up a light snack for the boys and the coaches. She just happened to have a whole roasted turkey in the refrigerator and a bunch of frozen hamburger patties that she thawed out in the microwave and fried in the cast-iron pan. She even had enough hamburger buns in the freezer to feed the first-string offensive and defensive teams and took care of the substitutes by scrambling three dozen eggs, cooking grits, and making homemade biscuits. She topped it off with six apple pies she had made and frozen—just in case anybody showed up.

Thelma said she wouldn't take any pay for all this, but she did tell the boys' coach that she could use some more trivets. For those of you who have spent most of your adult lives in Hardees and McDonald's, trivets are things that you set hot casserole dishes on to keep them from burning the tabletop.

Well, the Ware Shoals team went straight to shop class the next Monday and made Thelma thirty-eight trivets. Some of them were just circles of wood, which are fine, and others were fancy little platforms. I'm sorry you can't taste any of Thelma's chicken pot pie, but you can make her trivets.

WHAT YOU'LL NEED

- Two pieces of ¾ x 1 x 10-inch molding or other wood strip, preferably a hardwood
- Eight pieces of ½ x 1-inch strips of wood, also hardwood, like maple or oak

- One small box of 6-penny finishing nails
- One small bottle of wood glue

HOW TO MAKE IT

Space the eight strips of wood across the two legs, spread a little glue, and nail in place. If you want to make it a little fancier, trace a pattern on the bottom strips with one of those plastic curves that the kids use in school and cut with a jigsaw. Sand and rub with a finishing oil, like tung oil, to preserve the natural grain of the wood. If you don't have a Thelma in your family, go ahead and make a batch of these anyway. They make great (inexpensive) presents, and I've never known a woman who turned down a trivet.

Norris Newton's Newspaper Recycling Bins

Ole Norris always was a thrifty soul, even when we were kids. Or maybe he was just a pack rat. He had giant balls of twine that he had saved over the years, along with containers of bottle caps, used stamps, rubber bands, and newspapers dating back to when Harry Truman was president. If recycling had been as popular then as it is now, Norris would have been a rich man. Not that he's hurting now. Norris hasn't done badly since he took a correspondence course on how to be a part-time rural mail carrier and postal clerk. He said the course work was pretty strenuous and involved long periods of sitting on a stool absolutely motionless while lots of people lined up for stamps. Then he said he had to learn to move much more slowly than he was used to. When he first started the course, he could tear off fourteen postage stamps and make change in just under forty-five seconds. By the time he graduated, he was up to four and one-half minutes.

Being a fill-in rural letter carrier has fit right in with Norris's career plans, too, since he now has lots of time to pick up aluminum cans and old newspapers for recycling. That, plus the admission he charges Yankee tourists to see the Southeast's Largest Ball of String, has earned him quite a comfortable living.

*　　*　　*

WHAT YOU'LL NEED

- One 48 x 48-inch sheet of ½-inch plywood
- Wood glue
- 3-penny finishing nails

HOW TO MAKE IT

Cut four pieces 6 x 12 inches; cut four pieces 7 x 12 inches; cut four pieces 5½ x 7 inches; and cut one piece 12 x 15 inches.

Put a bead of glue along the edges of two of the end panels and nail together to form one corner; now do the other two end panels the same way.

On the 12 x 15-inch bottom panel, glue the 5½ x 7-inch pieces on each corner. (This leaves a groove in the shape of a cross that allows a place for the twine to run beneath the newspapers.) Now attach the corners to the bottom with glue and nails.

Make as many of these as you need, and help Norris Newton save a tree. It's a shame you can't help him deliver mail. Maybe then I would have gotten my *Sports Illustrated* swimsuit issue in February instead of the week after the Fourth of July.

Monroe's Made-in-the-Shade Sunshade

Poor Monroe. After spending his formative years in the suburbs of Plum Branch, he married a city girl from Atlanta and immediately moved into the suburbs where the biggest tree was about the same size as his Labrador retriever, Rhett.

"There aren't any shade trees," Monroe complained to his new bride, Mandi.

"Oh, those little trees will grow faster than you can imagine," Mandi said. "Besides, I like the wallpaper in the kitchen and I just *lo-oov-vvve* that bay window."

"We don't have any limbs to hang a rope swing on," Monroe complained, inspecting one of the three saplings in the back yard.

"Silly," said Mandi, who sunbathes every day and has a tan that makes George Hamilton look washed out. "I don't know why you're so hung up over trees. All they do is block out the sun."

Well, Monroe couldn't explain it properly, mainly because he was still on his honeymoon and all the blood had rushed from his brain; but anybody who grew up in the country knows the importance of shade trees. Or more specifically, shade. Air conditioning was a novelty in the South until a few decades ago, so farmers and other folks who worked outside had to find relief from the sun any way they could. If there was a big oak tree, that's where you sat while you rested and waited for a breeze. Or if there were no trees, you tried to make the mule stand still so you could sit down in his shadow.

These are modern times, however, and even the most affluent suburbanite does not have mules. They have patios and sunshades. A sunshade does not block out the sunlight completely—build a shed if you want total shade—but it diffuses the sunlight. (That means it breaks it up, Lamar, so you don't get scorched by direct sunbeams.)

What Monroe did after Mandi left him for a lifeguard at Lake Lanier was to build a sunshade using lattice fence panels. You've seen them at the building supply places. They're usually 4 x 8 feet and come in treated and un-treated forms. Lamar measured the distance around his patio, dug a 24-inch hole at each corner, and planted four 4 x 4-inch treated posts, squared them up, and poured some quick-setting concrete around their bases. Then he nailed 2 x 6-inch supports around the top and then nailed 2 x 4-inch rafters longways every 24 inches and laid the lattice panels on top. Then he nailed them to the rafters using 8-penny galvanized nails. When you're nailing in the rafters, make sure they are positioned so there's room to lap the lattice panel halfway over each rafter so the panels will meet. Afterward, get a paint sprayer, and paint the lattice and frame a nice redwood color or whatever shade your wife tells you will match the house.

If, however, you want something a little more challeng-ing, here is a plan that Monroe would have used if he hadn't pawned all of his power tools to buy a Juice Tiger juicing machine and a complete set of Slim Whitman's albums. That's the problem with staying up late and watching all those TV commercials. By the way, Monroe says Slim Whitman's rendition of "La Paloma Blanca"

sounds a lot better if you run a few bunches of carrots through the Juice Tiger while the record's playing.

WHAT YOU'LL NEED

First, measure your patio to determine how large to make your sunshade. The one below is for Monroe's patio. Yours may be larger, which is probably one reason Mandi left Monroe two days after the honeymoon.

- Four 10-foot treated 4 x 4 posts for support
- Forty (more or less) 10-foot treated 2 x 2 slats
- Five 8-foot treated 2 x 4 boards for braces
- Four 8-foot treated 2 x 6 boards for rafters
- One 10-foot treated 2 x 6 board for a beam

- Two 12-foot treated 2 x 6 boards for ends
- Sixteen ⅜ x 3½-inch carriage bolts and nuts and washers
- Twelve ⅜ x 5½-inch carriage bolts and nuts and washers
- A couple of pounds of 16-penny common galvanized nails
- Three or four pounds of 10-penny decking nails (spiral)

HOW TO MAKE IT

If you have a concrete patio, dig four holes for your posts about 24 inches deep, or until your teenage son gets tired. They should be 12 feet apart on two sides and 8 feet, 3 inches on the other two sides, if you're following Monroe's measurements. As I said, you have to determine what size you need and adjust the measurements accordingly. Put a layer of gravel in the bottom, set the posts in the holes, and pack with dirt or fill with quick-setting concrete. Before the concrete sets, however, make sure the posts are straight and the lineup is square. If you have a wooden deck, you can connect the posts to the edge of your deck with a post anchor. In that case, you can get by using 8-foot 4 x 4s.

Get somebody to help you, preferably someone reliable, unlike your wife or son who wanders off to do something else at the wrong time. Attach the 2 x 6-inch boards to the posts by driving 16-penny nails about ¾ of the way in to hold them in place until you can drill a couple of ⅜-inch holes through the post and beam. Insert carriage bolts and tighten; then pull out the nails. Before putting up the rafters and middle beam, you need to borrow a saber saw or a handsaw and cut out a 1½-inch notch 2¾ inches deep 36 inches from each end of the middle beam. Cut similar notches in the rafters 48 inches from the end so the notches line up, making a smooth, flat surface to place the slats.

Any problem so far? You might have to use a chisel to square up the notches, but keep working with them until the rafters and beams fit properly. Now get your helper to hold the beam in place while you nail it with 16-penny nails, and then place the rafters across it and nail them to the other beams.

Make the braces by mitering the ends at 45 degrees and cutting about 31½ inches long. You'll need eight of these, along with eight 2 x 4-inch blocks for cleats (See drawing). Attach the braces to the 2 x 6-inch beams with 3½-inch carriage bolts, and nail the other ends to the post and the cleats with 16-penny nails.

Now you're ready to put the slats on top. Use a 2-inch block or a 1½-inch block as a guide to keep the spacing between each slat consistent, and nail the slats into place using the 10-penny spiral nails.

All that's left to do now is sweep up the debris, set up your picnic table, and fire up the grill. You've got it made in the shade.

Lamar's Livestock and
Small Animal Holding Pens

I realize that not everybody's zoning laws or neighborhood covenants are as liberal as those in Lamar's hometown of Persimmon Branch. In Persimmon Branch, pigs and other livestock are not only permitted, they are strongly recommended. The chamber of commerce's motto is: Show us a household without a goat, and we'll show you an uppity Yankee family.

Lamar's menagerie is not as large as it used to be before he was laid off from the mill three years ago. Pinky was the first to go, followed in quick succession by Porky, Panky, and Piglet. Now he's down to a one-eyed shoat, two goats, and a three-legged chicken. The latter is the sole remnant of an interesting experiment that Lamar tried a few months ago. You see, Lamar grew up in a reasonably large family, and since he was the youngest, there usually were not any fried chicken drumsticks left for him at Sunday dinner. That's when Lamar got the idea of working with one of the eccentric former professors from Clemson University's poultry science department to develop chickens with three legs.

Things worked amazingly well at first. By injecting pullets with extra drumstick chromosomes, they were able to come up with four chickens that had three legs. Then the professor lost interest and moved to Alabama, where he is working on developing a faster strain of opossum.

A tourist passing by Lamar's house one day was amazed to see this chicken running alongside his car at thirty miles an hour. He speeded up to forty, then fifty, and the chicken simply ran faster until it passed the car and turned into Lamar's driveway. The tourist stopped, knocked on the door, and asked Lamar if he was aware that his chicken had three legs.

"Yep," Lamar said. "Raise 'em for their drumsticks."

"That's fascinating," the tourist said. "Well, tell me, do they taste any different from ordinary chickens?"

"Don't know," Lamar said, squinting into the noonday sun. "Never have been able to catch one."

Well, if Lamar had built the proper poultry pens, he wouldn't have had that problem. You may not have any three-legged chickens, but chances are you have cats, dogs, rabbits, guinea pigs, or some such pets. Why keep them cooped up in those cramped, store-bought cages when you can keep them cooped up in spacious home-made accommodations?

Here are a couple of project ideas:

A Doghouse

Dogs are not very picky about their housing or their food, except for those miniature yapping poodles or some kind of lap dog. Then they will only eat sautéed sweet-breads in champagne sauce and rare prime rib.

WHAT YOU'LL NEED
- Three sheets of ¾-inch exterior grade plywood
- 2 8-foot 2 x 2 boards
- One 10-foot 2 x 4 board
- A box of 1½-inch drywall screws
- A handful of 8-penny finishing nails

HOW TO MAKE IT

Cut the front piece about 36 inches high and 30 inches wide, depending on the size of your dog. Mark off a door, either a square or a nice rounded opening, and cut out with a saber saw or a jigsaw.

Cut the back piece 30 inches wide by 32 inches high. Now cut the roof 34 inches wide by 42 inches long. Tack lightly on top of the back and front pieces, getting your wife or son to help you hold them upright and marking off a 4-inch overhang on the front and 2-inch overhang at the rear. Use 8-penny finishing nails, and drive them in only about halfway. This is so you can cut your sides and mark the right angle. For the sides, cut two pieces 36 x 36 inches, and hold them against the sides. Mark the top with a pencil for the proper angle from front to back and cut the side pieces. Now cut the 2 x 2s for corner braces. Two will be slightly less than 32 inches high (for the back), and two will be slightly less than 36 inches high (for the front). Attach sides, front, back, and roof section with drywall screws (if you have a variable speed drill with a screwdriver attachment, it's a whole lot easier).

Build the floor by cutting another piece of plywood slightly larger than the doghouse (so your dog will have a little ledge) and cut three pieces of 2 x 4 the same width. Attach with drywall screws, place in the location where you want the doghouse, and set the house on top of it. If you're worried about it sliding off, toenail a few 8-penny finishing nails around the outside. Add a hot tub, a wet bar, and a Milk-Bone, and Rover will be happy. Of course, Lamar made his much bigger (about 10 x 12 feet) and put in an old sofa, a porta-potty, a small refrigerator, and that picture of dogs playing poker that you see everywhere. Lamar says if you have to spend time in the doghouse, you might as well be comfortable.

A Cat House

Follow the same plan for the doghouse, except add a scratching post, a potty box, and a large boulder that can be pushed up against the door to prevent escape. Cats don't like to stay anywhere that is not centrally heated and doesn't have a reasonably new sofa, and they have been known to crawl through openings too small for a mouse.

Big Barb's Breakfast Tray

Big Barb (not to be confused with Little Barb, her daughter, who is an Avon lady in Greenwood) was born to live a life of leisure. Unfortunately, she married Herb Stratton, the midnight shift delivery man for Krispy Dunk Do-Nuts. Not only has Herb's salary not kept up with Barb's expectations, but neither has his ardor. It takes a lot out of a man when he has to sleep in the daytime and work at night. So what Big Barb does is stay up late watching old movies and eating day-old doughnuts until Herb comes home around 9:00 A.M. with a fresh, warm batch.

But the fact that Herb is not a tiger in the bedroom doesn't mean he's not romantic. On their fourth anniversary, just after Big Barb was thrown out of Weight Watchers for smuggling a variety bucket of Kentucky Fried Chicken into the weekly meeting, Herb made her a breakfast tray. Every Sunday morning Herb brings Big Barb a romantic breakfast in bed (country fried steak, cream gravy, cathead biscuits, and cheese grits) along with a single rose. Herb may not have provided the kind of home Big Barb wanted (he just got around to underpinning their double-wide last October), but he knows how to make her happy.

So has the romance gone out of your marriage? Has the spark disappeared from your sex life? Maybe you should build a Big Barb breakfast tray. What you put on it is nobody's business but your own.

WHAT YOU'LL NEED

- Two pieces of 1 x 4 x 16-inch pine or a nice hardwood, like maple (if you want to spend that much)
- One piece of ¼ x 13½-inch sanded plywood
- Two pieces of 1 x 6 x 15-inch pine or hardwood
- One small bottle of wood glue
- One small box of 4-penny finishing nails
- One pint of stain
- One pint of polyurethane satin or gloss

HOW TO MAKE IT

All Herb did with Big Barb's tray was to nail the bottom to the two end pieces, but you don't want to be that sloppy. Lay out a mark about ¾ inch from the bottom of your end pieces and ¾ inch in from each side. Using a ¼ inch straight-cut bit in your neighbor's router (and have the router mounted in the router stand), route a groove about ¼ inch deep on each end piece. Not all the way across, now. Stop it ¾ inch from each side and using a ¼ inch chisel, make the groove square so the plywood bottom will slip into it on each end.

Make the holes for the handles by drilling two holes 5 inches apart and using a jigsaw to cut a ¾-inch slot. Round the edges as much as possible with the jigsaw and then sand.

Now fit the bottom piece into the slots and nail in place with 4-penny finishing nails after applying a thin bed of glue.

Attach the sides with finishing nails (use a nailset to drive them below the surface, and fill in the holes with plastic wood).

Round off the corners with a belt sander, apply a coat or two of stain and polyurethane, a you're ready to serve your loved one a big plate of eggs and grits or some other romantic repast.

Jim Frank's Foot Stool

If Jim Frank Morton is not the laziest man in McCormick County, South Carolina, he has a lock on second place. Ever since Jim Frank's wife Ovaltine bought him a La-Z-Boy recliner and a remote control TV for Christmas, the only exercise Jim Frank gets is when he lifts up the sofa cushions to look for loose change or spilled Doritos. Jim Frank used to be in charge of monitoring the water pressure at the pump station, but the stress proved to be too much and he took medical disability. That was fourteen years ago. Since then, he makes couch potatoes look like Jane Fonda during one of her step aerobic workouts.

Speaking of step aerobics, Ovaltine decided one day to build a footstool for Jim Frank in hopes that maybe he would step up and down on it for a few minutes a day just to get a little exercise. All of her friends told her this was nothing but wishful thinking, since the last strenuous activity Jim Frank undertook was cranking the satellite dish by hand after the motor was knocked out during a lightning storm. And he wouldn't have done that if the Braves hadn't been playing the Dodgers.

Although Ovaltine is pretty handy with tools, this footstool is reasonably easy to make.

WHAT YOU'LL NEED

- One piece of ¾ x 8½ x 19-inch pine board for the top
- Two pieces of ¾ x 4 x 16¾-inch pine boards for the sides
- Two pieces of ¾ x 8½ x 12-inch pine boards for the legs
- One small box of 2-inch drywall screws

HOW TO MAKE IT

Cut your pieces to size on your neighbor's table saw with an 80-degree angle for the legs at top and bottom so they will be positioned slightly spread out for better stability. Cut a 4-inch slot on each side of the legs to accommodate the side braces. Now cut a little decorative notch in the bottom of the legs about three or four inches deep.

Drill ⅙-inch pilot holes for your screws, and attach the top and sides. Use a saber saw or a belt sander to round out the corners. If you want this to be fancy, and Ovaltine did, countersink your screws and fill in with plastic wood. Sand, stain, and finish with a coat of polyurethane.

I hope you are as pleased with your footstool as Jim Frank has been with his. Not only does he use it to prop up his feet when the La-Z-Boy is in the shop, he finds it is real handy for standing on to see if there are any more jars of peanuts on the top shelf of Ovaltine's pantry.

Patti's Patio Bench

Patti says the best thing Snooker ever did for her was to build her a patio and leave a stack of 2 x 4s before running off with Beauty Simmons from the Little Egypt Truck Stop. That's about *all* that Snooker ever did for her. Snooker ran Jim Frank a close race in the lazy competition, but at least Snooker would rouse himself out of bed before noon to go play a couple of hours of pool. Then he'd swing by the sewing plant at the end of the first shift to pick up Patti in time to take her to her second job as a waitress at José's South of the Border Chinese restaurant (It was fine with the locals, but tourists who had actually eaten authentic Mexican and Chinese food never could get used to egg rolls stuffed with refried beans and guacamole and sweet and sour tacos).

After eleven years of this, Patti began to consider a divorce, but Snooker saved her the trouble by leaving town with Beauty Simmons, who he mistakenly thought was a mattress heiress. As soon as Beauty's tax refund check is gone, Patti expects Snooker will come crawling back asking for forgiveness.

In the meantime, she's been enjoying her patio by sitting on her patio bench, sipping margaritas, listening to Jimmy Buffett records, and watching the fire ants build new mounds. It could be worse, she says. She could be in the tropics where life is really dull. And she could be there with Snooker.

Anyway, if you'd like a nice patio bench like Patti's, here's all you have to do:

WHAT YOU'LL NEED

- Seven pieces of 1 x 3 x 42-inch treated wood or red-wood (for the seat)
- Three pieces of 2 x 4 x 40-inch treated wood or red-wood (for the lengthwise pieces of the frame)
- Four pieces of 2 x 4 x 20-inch treated wood or red-wood (for the horizontal end pieces)
- Four pieces of 2 x 4 x 18-inch treated wood or red-wood (for the vertical end pieces)
- One small box of 6-penny galvanized finishing nails
- One small box of 1¾-inch drywall screws

- One small bottle of waterproof glue
- One quart paint or water seal

HOW TO MAKE IT

Prepare the frame by cutting lap joints for the side pieces (that's where you cut half the thickness of each piece to fit the width of the piece). Assemble using drywall screws and glue. Add cross brace at top and bottom brace (lengthwise) and attach with glue and screws.

Using a $9/16$-inch (or a $1/2$-inch) block as a spacer, attach the 1 x 3s to the top of the frame with the finishing nails and glue.

Sand and stain treated wood or use a waterproof sealer on redwood. Sand the corners and edges with a belt sander until they are rounded, and you're ready to have a seat.

Denise's Deck Table for One

Denise is not exactly what you'd call an old maid, although she's pushing thirty-two and has never been seriously interested in anyone since Charles Coatsworth. Folks in Plum Branch say that experience left a bad taste in Denise's mouth, which is probably an understatement. Denise was teaching eighth-grade math at the middle school when she met Charles, who was teaching home ec. That should have been a tipoff right there, but Denise was blinded by love. Everything was proceeding smoothly until about two days before the wedding. That's when

WASTIN' AWAY IN MARGARITA-VILLE...

Charles announced that he had to call off the ceremony because he had to undergo some minor surgery.

As it turned out, the surgery wasn't so minor. Charles is now Charlayne and is part owner of a poodle grooming business in Sandy Springs. Denise, who always hated poodles, bought a beagle and built a deck on the back of what was to have been their dream house. Even that hasn't worked out. Blubber the Beagle got run over by the Roto-Rooter truck and the mosquitoes have been so bad this summer that Denise has had to eat inside. As soon as it gets cooler, though, and the bugs go away, she plans on using her deck table for one. If this story has really boosted your spirits to the point that you'd like a table, too, go ahead. It's easy to make.

WHAT YOU'LL NEED

- Four pieces of 2 x 4 x 28-inch treated wood
- Four pieces of 2 x 4 x 21-inch treated wood
- Five pieces of 1 x 8 x 48-inch treated wood
- 10-penny galvanized nails (a couple of handfuls)

HOW TO MAKE IT

Nail the frame together with the 10-penny galvanized nails (or you can use 2-inch drywall screws).

Position each board on top of the frame and adjust until you have an equal amount of overhang on each side and an equal amount of overhang at each end. Nail in place with 10-penny nails. Round off corners with a belt sander, sand other rough edges, and then paint with a redwood stain or whatever color you like.